COMPUTERS
Simplified®
6TH EDITION

Visual

by Paul McFedries

WILEY

Wiley Publishing, Inc.

COMPUTERS SIMPLIFIED®, 6TH EDITION

Published by
Wiley Publishing, Inc.
111 River Street
Hoboken, NJ 07030-5774

Published simultaneously in Canada

Library of Congress Control Number: 2005931141

ISBN-13: 978-0-7645-9752-7

ISBN-10: 0-7645-9752-3

Manufactured in the United States of America

10 9 8 7 6 5 4 3 2

Contact Us

For general information on our other products and services please contact our Customer Care Department within the U.S. at 800-762-2974, outside the U.S. at 317-572-3993 or fax 317-572-4002.

For technical support please visit www.wiley.com/techsupport.

WILEY
Wiley Publishing, Inc.

Sales

Contact Wiley at (800) 762-2974 or fax (317) 572-4002.

Praise for Visual Books

"Like a lot of other people, I understand things best when I see them visually. Your books really make learning easy and life more fun."

John T. Frey (Cadillac, MI)

"I have quite a few of your Visual books and have been very pleased with all of them. I love the way the lessons are presented!"

Mary Jane Newman (Yorba Linda, CA)

"I just purchased my third Visual book (my first two are dog-eared now!), and, once again, your product has surpassed my expectations."

Tracey Moore (Memphis, TN)

"I am an avid fan of your Visual books. If I need to learn anything, I just buy one of your books and learn the topic it in no time. Wonders! I have even trained my friends to give me Visual books as gifts."

Illona Bergstrom (Aventura, FL)

"Thank you for making it so clear. I appreciate it. I will buy many more Visual books."

J.P. Sangdong (North York, Ontario, Canada)

"I have several books from the Visual series and have always found them to be valuable resources."

Stephen P. Miller (Ballston Spa, NY)

"Thank you for the wonderful books you produce. It wasn't until I was an adult that I discovered how I learn — visually. Nothing compares to Visual books. I love the simple layout. I can just grab a book and use it at my computer, lesson by lesson. And I understand the material! You really know the way I think and learn. Thanks so much!"

Stacey Han (Avondale, AZ)

"I absolutely admire your company's work. Your books are terrific. The format is perfect, especially for visual learners like me. Keep them coming!"

Frederick A. Taylor, Jr. (New Port Richey, FL)

"I have several of your Visual books and they are the best I have ever used."

Stanley Clark (Crawfordville, FL)

"I bought my first Visual book last month. Wow. Now I want to learn everything in this easy format!"

Tom Vial (New York, NY)

"Thank you, thank you, thank you...for making it so easy for me to break into this high-tech world. I now own four of your books. I recommend them to anyone who is a beginner like myself."

Gay O'Donnell (Calgary, Alberta, Canada)

"I write to extend my thanks and appreciation for your books. They are clear, easy to follow, and straight to the point. Keep up the good work! I bought several of your books and they are just right! No regrets! I will always buy your books because they are the best."

Seward Kollie (Dakar, Senegal)

"Compliments to the chef!! Your books are extraordinary! Or, simply put, extra-ordinary, meaning way above the rest! THANK YOU THANK YOU THANK YOU! I buy them for friends, family, and colleagues."

Christine J. Manfrin (Castle Rock, CO)

"What fantastic teaching books you have produced! Congratulations to you and your staff. You deserve the Nobel Prize in Education in the Software category. Thanks for helping me understand computers."

Bruno Tonon (Melbourne, Australia)

"Over time, I have bought a number of your 'Read Less - Learn More' books. For me, they are THE way to learn anything easily. I learn easiest using your method of teaching."

José A. Mazón (Cuba, NY)

"I am an avid purchaser and reader of the Visual series, and they are the greatest computer books I've seen. The Visual books are perfect for people like myself who enjoy the computer, but want to know how to use it more efficiently. Your books have definitely given me a greater understanding of my computer, and have taught me to use it more effectively. Thank you very much for the hard work, effort, and dedication that you put into this series."

Alex Diaz (Las Vegas, NV)

Credits

Project Editor
Jade L. Williams

Acquisitions Editor
Jody Lefevere

Product Development
Manager
Lindsay Sandman

Copy Editor
Marylouise Wiack

Technical Editor
Namir Shammas

Editorial Manager
Robyn Siesky

Manufacturing
Allan Conley
Linda Cook
Paul Gilchrist
Jennifer Guynn

Illustrations
Steven Amory
Matthew Bell
Ronda David-Burroughs
Cheryl Grubbs
Sean Johanessen
Jacob Mansfield
Rita Marley
Elizabeth Cardenas-Nelson
Paul Schmitt

Book Design
Kathie S. Rickard

Production Coordinator
Nancee Reeves

Layout
Kathie S. Rickard
Amanda Spagnuolo

Screen Artwork
Jill A. Proll

Proofreader
Christine Pingleton

Quality Control
Brian H. Walls

Indexer
Steve Rath

Vice President and
Executive Group Publisher
Richard Swadley

Vice President and
Publisher
Barry Pruett

Composition Director
Debbie Stailey

About the Author

Paul McFedries is the president of Logophilia Limited, a technical writing company. While now primarily a writer, Paul has worked as a programmer, consultant, and Web site developer. Paul has written more than 40 books that have sold over three million copies worldwide. These books include the Wiley titles *Teach Yourself VISUALLY Windows XP, Second Edition*, and *Windows XP Top 100 Simplified Tips and Tricks, Second Edition*.

Author's Acknowledgments

The book you hold in your hands is not only an excellent learning tool, but it is truly beautiful, as well. I am happy to have supplied the text that you will read, but the gorgeous images and the layout of the tasks come from Wiley's crack team of artists and illustrators. The accuracy of the spelling and grammar, and the veracity of the information are all the result of hard work performed by project editor Jade Williams, copy editor Marylouise Wiack, and technical editor Namir Shammas. Thanks to all of you for your excellent work. My thanks, as well, to acquisitions editor Jody Lefevere for bringing me onboard.

Table of Contents

4

Getting Started with Your Computer

5

Learning Windows XP Basics

Table of Contents

Table of Contents

Chapter 1

Getting Familiar with Computer Basics

Are you ready to start learning about computers? This chapter will help by introducing you to the computer and showing you its benefits and uses. You learn about the different types of computers, take a tour of a typical personal computer, and learn the difference between computer hardware and software.

Discover the Computer

A computer is a device that you can use to store, manipulate, and display text, numbers, images, and sounds.

Computer

A *computer* is an electronic device that is designed to work with information. The computer takes information in, processes that information, and then displays the results. In this way, a computer is similar to a calculator, except that even the smallest computer is much more versatile than the most powerful calculator. Computers operate at amazingly fast speeds, with a typical computer processing millions of calculations every second.

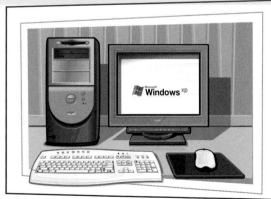

Personal Computer

A *personal computer* is a small, relatively inexpensive computer that is designed for use by one person at a time. It allows you to perform personal tasks such as creating documents, communicating with other people, and playing games. The abbreviation *PC* is most often used to refer to computers that run the Microsoft Windows operating system, as well as to differentiate them from Macintosh computers.

Benefits of Using a Computer

A computer is a powerful and useful tool because it gives you a number of benefits, including the ability to quickly produce high-quality work.

It also enables you to learn new skills that are an important part of today's technological world.

Speed

Computers allow you to perform many everyday tasks more quickly. For example, if you mail a letter to a friend, he may receive it in a few days. However, if you e-mail him, he receives your message in a few minutes. Similarly, if you manually compose a newsletter, it may take you a week, whereas using a computer, it may take just an afternoon.

Quality

The tools that come with a computer enable you to create high-quality documents and drawings, even if you are not a typesetter or an artist. With just a few simple techniques, you can create documents that look professional or are exactly suited to your present task.

New Skills

Because we live in a computer age, basic computer skills are often required to accomplish many daily tasks. Typing on a keyboard, using a mouse, and other basic computer skills are useful in many different situations and are often required by employers.

What You Can Do with a Computer

Most electronic devices — such as DVD players, camcorders, and personal stereos — only do one thing. However, because computers are versatile by design, they enable you to do many things.

For example, you can use a computer to listen to music, watch movies, create flyers, research your family history, educate your children, and play games.

Create Documents

You can use your computer to create letters, resumes, memos, reports, newsletters, brochures, business cards, menus, flyers, invitations, and certificates. Anything that you use to communicate on paper, you can create using your computer.

Monitor Your Finances

You can use your computer to perform basic financial management. For example, you can create a budget, record expenses, balance your checkbook, calculate your taxes, and monitor your mortgage. If you run a small business, then you can allocate income and expenses, create financial reports, and calculate your profit and loss.

Perform Research

You can use your computer and the Internet to research almost any topic that you can think of. For example, you can learn more about a vacation destination, trace your family history, access back issues of newspapers and magazines, and compare product features before you buy them.

Work with Numbers

You can use a spreadsheet program to work with numbers on your computer. For example, you can create a mortgage amortization schedule, calculate how much money you need to save for retirement, monitor an investment portfolio, and create a business plan.

Store Data

You can use your computer, and the appropriate software, to store and work with large amounts of data. You can track personal items such as CDs, recipes, contact information for friends and relatives, and fitness activities. For business, you can track clients and potential clients, inventory, products, and orders.

Schedule Your Time

You can use your computer as an electronic day-timer to record upcoming activities, birthdays, anniversaries, events, meetings, and appointments. You can also set up some scheduling programs to remind you of approaching events so that you do not forget them.

Teach Your Children

You can use your computer to help educate your children. Many programs available are designed to assist children with reading, drawing, learning math and science, solving problems, and enhancing creativity.

continued

What You Can Do with a Computer *(continued)*

Learn New Life Skills

You can use your computer to learn new life skills. Programs are available that teach you how to speak a different language, play chess, cook, garden, design a home, play a musical instrument, and design and make clothes.

Make New Friends

You can use your computer and the Internet to enhance your social life. You can chat with other people by typing messages to them, join mailing lists, find support groups, find clubs and organizations in your area, and find a date.

Keep In Touch

You can use your computer to communicate with friends, family, colleagues, and clients that you do not often see face-to-face. You can send e-mail messages and instant messages, and you can even talk to another person using a microphone and your computer's speakers.

Buy and Sell

You can use your computer and the Internet to buy and sell things. Many online stores enable you to purchase anything, from books to baby accessories, and have it delivered to your door. There are also auction sites, such as eBay, that enable you to sell items that you create or that you no longer need.

Create Items

You can use your computer to bring out your creative side. For example, you can create your own greeting cards or wedding invitations, draw pictures, manipulate digital photos, edit digital movies, record sounds, and compose music.

Play Media

You can use your computer to play digital media, including music CDs, audio files, video files, animations, DVDs, music, and movies that you have downloaded from the Internet.

Play Games

You can use your computer to play many different types of games. You can solve a puzzle, fly a plane, race a car, go on an adventure, play football or hockey, battle aliens, plan a city, play backgammon or checkers, or deal poker.

Types of Computers

When selecting a computer that is best for your needs, you should consider what purpose it will serve in your home or business, and whether it should be mobile for travel.

Desktop

A *desktop* is by far the most common type of computer. Most desktop systems come with a separate computer case, monitor, keyboard, and mouse. On older desktops, the computer case lies flat on the desk with the monitor sitting on top. Almost all newer systems use a *tower* case that sits upright. You can place this case either on a desk or on the floor.

Notebook

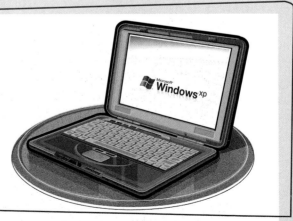

A *notebook* is a computer that combines the case, monitor, keyboard, and mouse in one unit. It is also called a *laptop* or a *portable*. Notebooks are light — usually only four to six pounds — so you can take them out of your office or home. Most notebooks are just as powerful as a desktop system.

Tablet PC

A *tablet PC* is a computer that looks similar to a small notebook. However, the tablet PC screen pivots so that it lies on top of the keyboard, making it look like a writing tablet. You can use a *digital pen* to input your data or select items on the screen.

Handheld PC

A *handheld PC* is a very small computer — usually weighing less than a pound — that you can hold comfortably in your hand or carry in a jacket pocket. A handheld PC is also called a *personal digital assistant* (PDA) or *palmtop*. Most people use a handheld PC to store their schedules and check their e-mail while out of the office.

Server

A *server* is a powerful computer that acts as a central resource for a number of other computers that are connected to it. These other computers can be desktops or stripped-down *terminals* that use the server to run programs and store data. Some servers are *mainframes*, which are giant computers that run large-scale operations, such as airline reservation systems.

Tour the Personal Computer

MAIN PERSONAL COMPUTER PARTS

Learning to use a personal computer is much easier if you know how a typical system is laid out and what each major part does.

Computer Case

The *computer case*, also called the *system unit* or *console*, holds the electronic chips and devices that make the computer work. The outside of the case has an on/off switch, and the rear of the case is where you plug in the other computer components. For more information about the internal components of your computer, see Chapter 2.

Monitor

The *monitor*, also called the *screen* or *display*, is a TV-like device that the computer uses to display text, images, and other information.

Keyboard

The *keyboard* is a typewriter-like device that you use to type information and enter instructions for the computer to follow. To learn how to work the keyboard, see Chapter 4.

Mouse

The *mouse* is a hand-operated pointing device that you use to select or move items on the screen, as well as to provide instructions for the computer to follow. To learn how to operate the mouse, see Chapter 4.

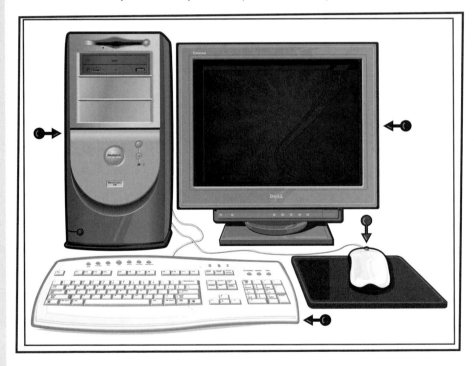

Printer

A *printer* is a device that you use to print a document from a computer. Some printers are *all-in-one* devices that can also fax, copy, and scan documents.

Speakers

The *speakers* are devices that output the sound effects, music, narration, and other audio that your computer generates. You can also use *headphones* so that only you can hear the computer's output.

Uninterruptible Power Supply

An *uninterruptible power supply* (UPS) is a device that provides temporary power to your computer should the electricity fail. This device enables you to shut down your computer properly to avoid losing data.

Game Controller

The *game controller* is a device that you can use to control the action in a computer game.

Surge Protector

A *surge protector* is a device that protects your computer from damage by power fluctuations, which are most often caused by lightning.

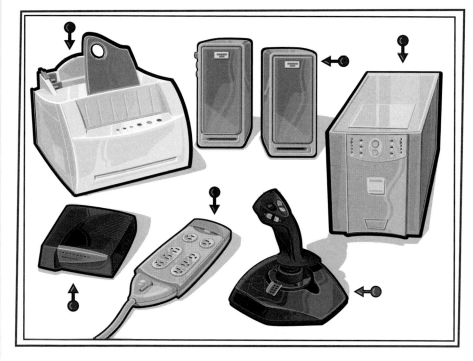

Modem

The *modem* is a device that connects your computer to the Internet, either through telephone lines or TV cable. Some modems, called internal modems, reside inside the computer case.

continued

Tour the Personal Computer *(continued)*

FRONT OF A PERSONAL COMPUTER CASE

On a typical personal computer, the front of the case contains a number of buttons, indicator lights and slots.

Power Switch

When the computer is off, press the *power switch* to turn the computer on. When you have finished working with your computer and have shut down all of your programs, press the power switch again to turn off the computer.

Reset Switch

You can press the *reset switch* to restart the computer when it is running. Keep in mind that you should only do this if your computer is frozen and no longer responds to your commands.

Activity Light

The *activity light* flashes on and off when your computer is performing a task, such as accessing the main hard disk.

Floppy Disk Drive

The *floppy disk drive* is a storage device that accepts *floppy disks*, which enable you to move files from one computer to another.

CD-ROM or DVD Drive

A *CD-ROM drive* is a storage device that accepts data CD-ROMs (compact discs), which resemble musical CD-ROMs. Most new computers also have a *DVD drive*, which accepts data DVDs. For more information, see Chapter 2.

PERSONAL COMPUTER PARTS

On a typical personal computer, the reart of the case contains a number of holes and slots, called parts, into which you plug computer devices.

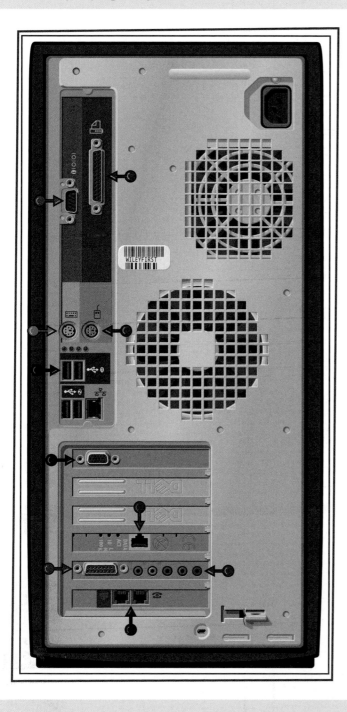

Monitor Port
You use the *monitor port* to plug in the monitor.

Keyboard Port
You use the *keyboard port* to plug in the keyboard.

Mouse Port
You use the *mouse port* to plug in the mouse.

Printer Port
You use the *printer port* to plug in the printer. This is also called a *parallel port*.

Serial Port
You use the *serial port* to plug in a dial-up modem, as well as some older versions of the mouse. This is also called a *COM port*.

USB Port
You use a *Universal Serial Bus* (USB) *port* to plug in a USB device. Many computer peripherals – including keyboards, mice, and printers – come in USB versions.

Sound Ports
You use the *sound ports* to plug in sound devices, such as your speakers (the green-colored port on most new systems) and microphone (the pink-colored port). Some systems also have Line In and Line Out ports that you can use to connect the computer to external audio equipment.

Modem Ports
You use the *modem ports* to connect your computer's internal modem to your telephone system.

Network Port
You use the *network port* to plug in a cable that connects either to a network or to a high-speed Internet modem. This is also called an *Ethernet port*.

Game Port
You use the *game port* to plug in a game controller.

Learn About Computer Hardware

Computer hardware consists of the physical components of your computer: the parts, devices, buttons, and ports that you can touch and physically manipulate.

Computer hardware comes in two basic varieties: external and internal.

External Hardware

External hardware, also known as *peripherals*, refers to hardware that connects to the outside of the computer case. The monitor, keyboard, and mouse are the most common external hardware devices. The printer and speakers are also popular peripherals. You can connect external hardware to your computer through the computer ports described on the previous page.

Internal Hardware

Internal hardware refers to hardware that resides inside the computer case. This includes the *central processing unit* (CPU), the brains of the computer, — *memory chips* that are used for temporary data storage while you work, *disk drives* that are used for long-term storage, and *circuit boards* that supply many of the ports on the back of the computer case. You can learn more about internal hardware devices in Chapter 2.

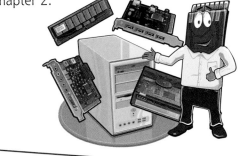

Explore Computer Software

Without software, your monitor would not display anything, your speakers would remain silent, and typing on the keyboard keys would have no effect. Computer software comes in two basic categories: application and system.

Computer software provides the instructions that enable the computer hardware to perform its tasks.

Application Software

Application software refers to the programs that you interact with to perform specific computer tasks. For example, a word-processing program enables you to create documents such as memos and letters, a graphics program enables you to draw an image, and an e-mail program enables you to send and receive e-mail messages.

System Software

System software refers to programs that operate behind the scenes to ensure that your computer system functions properly. This software is most often referred to as the *operating system*. Some examples of system software include Windows XP and Mac OS X. For more information about the operating system, see Chapter 2.

Chapter 2

Discovering How Your Computer Works

You do not need to become an electronics engineer to use your computer. However, it does help if you know at least a little bit about how your computer works, and what processes are going on internally when you work with your computer. This chapter introduces you to what you need to know.

Data Input Devices

Data input is the process of sending information to the computer. This information consists of either instructions for the computer or data that you want to store on the computer. This section introduces you to the main types of computer input devices.

Game Controller
A *game controller*, also called a *joystick*, is a device that you can use to control the action in a computer game. You can also use the joystick to provide instructions to the computer game, such as level and tool selection.

Document Scanner
A *document scanner* processes a document or photo much like a photocopier, except that a digital version of the scanned item is sent to the computer.

Digital Camera
You can use a *digital camera* to take pictures, which it then stores internally in digital form. You can then connect the camera to a computer and move the pictures from the camera to the computer.

Microphone
You can use a *microphone* to input your voice to a computer, either to provide instructions for the computer to follow or to record a narration.

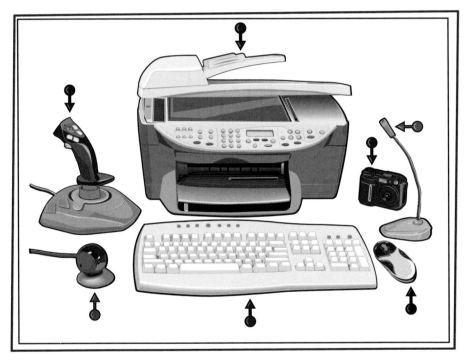

Mouse
When you move the *mouse* or press a mouse button, the action sends a signal along the mouse cable to the computer, and the operating system reacts accordingly.

Web Cam
A *Web cam* takes a series of pictures of a live scene and then saves the pictures on a computer. These pictures can be used on Web sites to monitor an area.

Keyboard
When you press a key on your *keyboard*, a signal that identifies that key travels through the keyboard cable to your computer. Depending on the key that you press, the operating system either displays a character or processes an instruction.

Data Output Devices

Data output refers to the movement of data from inside the computer to an output device, such as a monitor. This often occurs automatically because the computer has been programmed to display the results of certain operations. However, it can also occur at your request. This section introduces you to the main types of data output operations.

Display on a Monitor

Your monitor is your computerís most important output device. What you see on the screen is a reflection of what is happening inside the computer, and your programs display elements on the screen that enable you to control how the programs work. The screen also displays what you type, as well as your mouse movements.

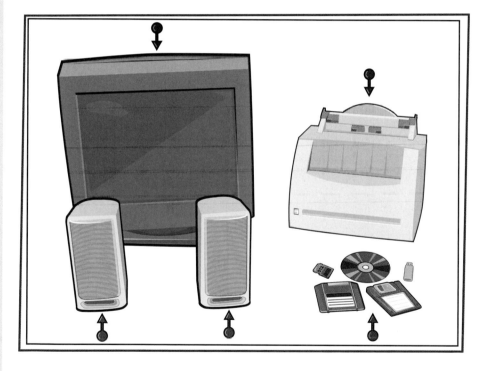

Print to a Printer

When you finish working with a document, you may want another person to view it. The easiest way to do that is to print the document on paper using your printer, and then give the resulting document, called a *hard copy*, to the other person.

Copy to a Disk

You can make a copy of a document and store it on media such as a floppy disk, CD-ROM or DVD disc, Zip disk, or memory card. This is useful for making backup copies of important documents or for sharing data with another person. For more information about data storage, see the section "Learn About Data Storage."

Play to Speakers

Your computer uses speakers for sound output. These speakers may be separate units, built into the monitor, or inside the computer case. If the system has an important message to display, the speakers may sound an alert to get your attention. You can use your speakers to play sound files, music CDs, and other audio data.

Learn About the Operating System

The operating system is the software that controls the overall operation of your computer. The operating system controls startup, application and hardware management, and shutdown.

Everything that happens on your computer is initiated, processed, and approved by the operating system, and so it is important that you understand how this software works. Windows XP and Mac OS X are two popular operating systems.

Startup

When you turn on your computer, the operating system immediately assumes control and prepares the computer for use. For example, it turns on devices such as the hard drive and floppy drive, and it runs various checks to ensure that the hardware is functioning properly. The operating system then displays the *interface*, the screen elements that you use to interact with your computer.

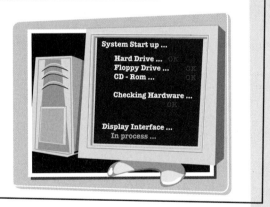

Files

One of the main functions of the operating system is to manage a computer's *files*. A file is an electronic collection of data and instructions that are stored as a unit. Your computer contains files that are used internally by your programs, as well as the documents, images, spreadsheets, and other data that you create. For more information about data storage, see the section "Learn About Data Storage."

Device Drivers

The operating system uses small programs called *device drivers* to communicate with your computer's hardware. For example, if you insert a CD-ROM, the operating system launches a device driver to read and display the contents of the disc.

Programs

The operating system interacts with your application software. For example, when you give the instruction to start a program, the operating system finds the appropriate files and opens them. The operating system also allocates computer resources, such as memory, to your programs.

Data Input

When you press a key on your keyboard, move your mouse, use a game controller, talk into your microphone, or start a document scan, the resulting input is first intercepted by the operating system. The system then directs the input appropriately — for example, relaying an instruction to a program or displaying a typed character on the screen.

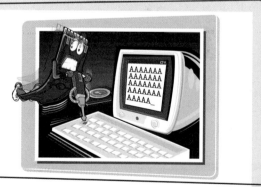

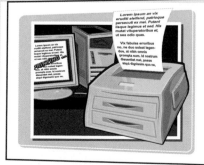

Data Output

When you request data output, the operating system responds to your request. For example, if you instruct a program to print a document, the operating system sends the document to the printer.

Tour the Central Processing Unit

The Central Processing Unit (CPU) is the computer's most important component because it handles, or directs, most of the tasks that occur inside the computer.

The CPU is also called the *microprocessor* or *processor*.

What Is a CPU?

A CPU is a *computer chip*, which is a piece of silicon that contains small electronic devices called *transistors*. These transistors contain components that are just .09 micron wide (an average human hair is 100 microns wide). The latest personal computer CPUs contain over 100 million transistors and can perform billions of instructions per second.

What a CPU Does

The purpose of the CPU is to coordinate the flow of data throughout the computer; this is why the CPU is often called the computer's brain. The CPU also performs math and logic calculations, sends data to and retrieves data from memory and storage devices, and processes hardware and software instructions.

CPU Manufacturers

The biggest manufacturer of CPUs is Intel, which makes the Pentium and Celeron processors. Other CPU manufacturers are: AMD, which manufactures the Sempron and Athlon chips; and VIA and Motorola, which manufacture the PowerPC chips used in Macs.

CPU speed

The most common measure of a CPU is its speed. The speed is measured in cycles per second (hertz or Hz), where a *cycle* represents a single task performed by the CPU, such as adding two numbers. CPU speeds are usually measured in gigahertz (GHz), or billions of cycles per second.

CPU Caches

Many CPUs come with a feature called a *cache*, which is a storage area where the CPU keeps frequently used data. This saves the CPU from having to extract that data from some more distant location in the computer's memory, thus improving computer performance. The latest CPUs have both a cache on the chip (usually called an *L1* cache) and a cache between the chip and memory (usually called an *L2* or *L3* cache) for maximum performance.

Front Side Bus

The average CPU spends much of its time transferring data to and from the computer's memory. The pathways on which this data travels are collectively called the *front side bus* (FSB), or simply the *bus*. The *FSB speed* determines how fast data travels between the CPU and memory. As a result, the faster the bus speed (usually measured in MHz — megahertz, or millions of cycles per second), the faster the computer performs. For more information about memory, see the section "Understanding Memory."

Understanding Memory

Memory is a temporary work area inside your computer. When you run a program or open a document, the operating system loads the corresponding files from your hard drive into memory.

RAM

ROM

Memory is like a carpenter's workshop: The raw materials are stored in another room, and the carpenter brings them into the workshop when they are needed. When the carpenter has completed the work, the finished piece is moved out of the workshop.

Memory and Performance

Because memory is where the computer holds your running programs and opens documents, the more memory you have, the more programs and documents you can have open. If you want to improve the performance of your computer, you can ask your local computer shop to add more memory to your system.

RAM Versus ROM

The memory that a computer uses as a temporary work area is also called *random access memory* (RAM), because the computer can randomly add data to and remove data from this memory. However, keep in mind that the data in RAM is erased when you turn off your computer. In contrast, *read-only memory* (ROM) stores data permanently, and you cannot change this data. For example, the instructions for initializing your computer's components when you turn the machine on are stored in ROM.

Memory Chip

RAM and ROM use special computer chips called *memory chips*. Each memory chip contains a large number of transistors that are designed to store computer data.

Memory Module

Computers do not use memory chips individually. Instead, the chips are attached to a special circuit board called a *memory module*. A *single inline memory module*, or SIMM, holds nine memory chips on one side of the board; a *dual inline memory module*, or DIMM, holds nine memory chips on each side of the board for a total of 18 chips. You can improve the performance and increase the speed of your system by adding more memory modules.

Measure Memory: Bits and Bytes

A memory chip stores data using tiny electronic devices that are either on or off. When the state of a device is on, it has a value of 1, and when the state is off, it has a value of 0. These values are called *bits*, which is short for binary digit. Characters, such as letters, numbers, and other symbols, are represented by 8-bit values, which are called *bytes*. For example, the letter *M* is represented by the following byte: 01001101.

Measure Memory: Kilobytes, Megabytes, and Gigabytes

A byte represents a single character of data. Because computers regularly deal with thousands and even millions of characters at a time, we need a system of measurement to represent these amounts. A *kilobyte* (KB) represents about 1,000 bytes (equivalent to about a page of text). A *megabyte* (MB) is about 1,000 kilobytes (equivalent to a thick book), and a *gigabyte* (GB) is about 1,000 megabytes (equivalent to a small library).

Learn About Data Storage

When you are finished working with your data, you can store it in a more permanent form on a hard drive or a removable drive.

Your computer's memory is only a temporary storage area for data.

Hard Drive

The *hard drive,* also called the *hard disk*, is your computer's main permanent storage area. The hard drive resides inside the computer case and stores your programs and documents. The hard drive is a magnetic disk that holds your data even when you turn off your computer. Most current hard drives can store many gigabytes of data.

External Hard Drive

Most computers contain a hard drive inside the computer case. However, you may want to add an additional hard drive to increase the storage space in your system. Because it can be difficult to install an internal hard drive, you may want to invest in an *external* hard drive, instead. An external hard drive remains outside of the computer case and attaches to one of the computer's ports, usually a USB port.

CD Drives

CD-ROM Drive

A *compact disc read-only memory* (CD-ROM) drive is one in which you insert a CD-ROM disc, which may contain data, software, or music. The ROM part of the drive name means that your computer can only read the disc's contents; it cannot change the contents.

CD-R Drive

A *compact disc-recordable* (CD-R) drive allows you to record, or *burn*, data to a CD-R disc. Keep in mind that you can only record data to the CD-R disc once. After that, you cannot change the disc's contents. CD-R drives can also read data from previously recorded CD-R discs, as well as from CD-ROM discs.

CD-RW Drive

A *compact disc-rewritable* (CD-RW) drive allows you to record data to a CD-RW disc. You can add data to, and erase data from, a CD-RW disc as often as you want. CD-RW drives can also read data from CD-R and CD-ROM discs.

CD Drive Speeds

CD drive performance is generally measured by how fast it is in three categories: *Write speed* determines how fast a CD-R drive records data; *Rewrite speed* determines how fast a CD-RW drive records data; *Read speed* determines how fast the drive reads a disc's contents. Speed is measured relative to a baseline amount. For example, a read speed of 56x means that the drive reads data 56 times faster than a music CD player.

continued

Learn About Data Storage *(continued)*

DVD-ROM Drive

A *digital versatile disc read-only memory* (DVD-ROM) drive allows you to use a DVD-ROM disc, which may contain data or software. The ROM part of the drive name means that your computer can only read the disc's contents; you cannot change the contents. All DVD drives can also read all CD-ROM, CD-R, and CD-RW discs.

DVD-R, DVD+R, or DVD±R Drive

A *digital versatile disc-recordable* (DVD-R, DVD+R, or DVD±R) drive allows you to record, or *burn,* data once to a DVD-R, DVD+R, or DVD±R disc. The ± symbol means that the drive supports both the DVD-R and DVD+R formats. DVD-R, DVD+R, and DVD±R drives can read data from previously recorded DVD-R, DVD+R, or DVD±R discs, as well as from DVD-ROM discs.

DVD-RW, DVD+RW, or DVD±RW Drive

A *digital versatile disc-rewritable* (DVD-RW, DVD+RW, or DVD±RW) drive allows you to record data to a DVD-RW, DVD+RW, or DVD±RW disc. You can add data to, and erase data from, the disc as often as you want.

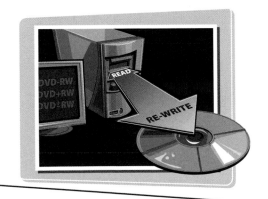

DVD Drive Speeds

DVD drive performance is generally determined by how fast it is in three categories: *Write speed* determines how fast a DVD-R, DVD+R, or DVD±R drive records data; *Rewrite speed* determines how fast a DVD-RW, DVD+RW, or DVD±RW drive records data; *Read speed* determines how fast the drive reads a disc's contents.

Secondary Types of Data Storage

Floppy Drive

A *floppy drive* is a device into which you insert a *floppy disk*. A floppy disk is a small (3.5 inches wide) magnetic disk that you can use to read and write data. Because floppy disks can only store about 1.44MB of data, they are not used very often these days. As a result, some computers, such as Macintosh, ship without a floppy drive.

Tape Drive

A *tape drive* is a device into which you insert a *tape cartridge*. A tape cartridge is similar to a cassette tape, except that a tape cartridge can store hundreds or even thousands of megabytes. Tape drives are most often used for making backups of your files. However, because large-capacity external hard drives are now more easily available, tape drives are becoming less popular.

Removable Storage

Removable storage refers to disks and cards that you can insert into and remove from special devices or ports that are attached to your computer. Popular examples include Zip disks, flash drives, and memory card formats such as CompactFlash, Memory Stick, and SecureDigital. You can use these disks with devices such as digital cameras, music players, cellular phones, and handheld computers.

Memory Card Reader

With so many different memory card formats available, companies are now producing multifunction *memory card readers* that have separate slots for each supported format. You can connect the reader to your computer's USB port and then insert a memory card into the appropriate slot.

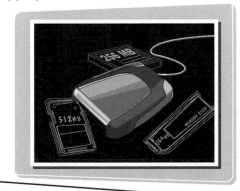

Purchasing a Computer

Before you purchase a computer, you need to know what type of computer is right for you and what extras you really need. This chapter helps you do that by explaining the sales jargon and demystifying the process of buying a computer.

4 sale

Choose a Computer Type

The most important consideration when purchasing a computer is the type of system that you need.

Desktop

Most computer users buy desktops because these systems offer the most flexible configurations. If your budget is limited, then you can purchase a less powerful system with fewer features; if money is not an issue, then you can purchase a high-performance computer with many features.

Notebook

Whether you travel for business or just want to work in the local coffee shop for a while, a notebook computer offers the flexibility to work almost anywhere. Keep in mind that a notebook generally costs more than the equivalent desktop computer.

Tablet PC

Choose a tablet PC if you often take notes at meetings and you want a convenient way to save those notes on your computer. The tablet PC's digital pen enables you to draw diagrams, annotate documents, and input handwritten messages.

Handheld PC

A handheld PC is useful if you need to be mobile both in and out of the office, because it enables you to keep your contacts and your schedule with you at all times. It also enables you to check e-mail when you are within range of a wireless Internet connection.

Select a CPU

In computer ads, the CPU is usually the first component that is mentioned, so it is important to understand what to look for, including the CPU type and speed. You should also understand the minimum CPU requirement of your operating system and what cache memory is installed on the CPU.

CPU Type

If you do not need a powerful computer, look for a system with an Intel Celeron processor. For a more powerful computer, look for an Intel Pentium 4 or AMD Sempron or Athlon processor. If you want to use a notebook on a wireless network, look for a processor that also comes with Intel's Centrino technology.

CPU Speed

Generally, the slower the CPU speed, the less expensive and less powerful the computer is. If you want to use your computer for basic activities, such as writing letters or memos, sending e-mails, and surfing the World Wide Web, then you do not need the fastest available processor. Any of today's processors should be fast enough for you.

Minimum CPU Requirements

If you plan to use Windows XP as your operating system, you need a CPU with a speed of at least 233 MHz. For Mac OS X, you need a PowerPC G3, G4, or G5.

Cache Memory

Cache memory can greatly improve the performance of a CPU, although the more memory on the chip, the more expensive a system is. If the ad only uses the word *cache*, it usually refers to the L2 cache, which can range from 256MB in less expensive systems, up to 2GB in high-end systems.

Determine How Much RAM You Need

The amount of random access memory (RAM) in your computer determines how fast your computer runs and what types of programs you can use.

Minimum Requirements

Every operating system has a minimum amount of RAM that it requires so that it can operate. For Windows XP, the minimum is 64MB; for Mac OS X, the minimum is 128MB.

Real-World Minimum Requirements

For day-to-day work, the suggested RAM minimums for Windows XP and Mac OS X are far too small. For both operating systems, your computer will perform much better if it has at least 256MB of RAM.

Multitasking Requirements

Both Windows XP and Mac OS X enable you to run multiple programs at the same time; a feature called *multitasking*. If you plan to run four or five (or more) programs at once, which is not unusual, then you need more memory in your system — at least 512MB.

Graphics and Database Requirements

If you plan to use programs that manipulate digital photos, edit digital videos, or work with extremely large files such as databases, then you need even more RAM — 1GB should be more than enough.

Select Data Storage Options

When buying a computer, you can choose the size of the hard drive as well as the other data storage options. The decisions that you make are important because they determine how you will store data on your computer.

Minimum Hard Drive Size

Windows XP requires at least 1.5GB of free space on your hard drive; for Mac OS X, the minimum free space required is 2GB. To load additional programs and data, you need at least a 4GB drive. If you plan on working with digital photos, videos, or music, get the largest hard drive you can afford — preferably 80GB or larger.

Hard Drive Performance

Rotational speed refers to how fast the hard drive platters rotate. A low-end hard drive may spin at 5,400 revolutions per minute (RPM), where as better drives rotate at 7,200 or even 10,000 RPM. *Seek time* refers to the average time that it takes to read and write data on the hard drive. Good hard drives have seek times of around 8.5 milliseconds (ms) or lower.

CD or DVD Drive

If you do not plan to view DVD movies or use DVD-based software, you can save money by getting just a CD-ROM drive, or a CD-R or CD-RW drive if you want to burn your own CDs. If you require DVD support, DVD-ROM drives are the least expensive choice. If you also want recording capabilities, you can buy a DVD±R or DVD±RW drive.

Built-In Memory Card Reader

Many computers now have memory card readers that are built into the front of the computer case. If you use multiple memory card formats, consider purchasing a system that has a built-in reader that supports the formats that you use.

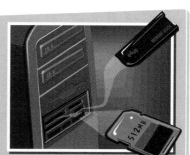

Choose a Monitor and Video Card

Because you look at the monitor all day long, you should get a good monitor/video card combination that is easy on your eyes and does not break your budget.

Monitor Type

There are two types of monitors available: A *cathode ray tube* (CRT) is the traditional monitor type and tends to be large, but inexpensive; a *liquid crystal display* (LCD, also called a *flat panel*) is the most recent monitor type. An LCD is smaller, sharper, and more expensive than a CRT.

Monitor Size

A large monitor allows you to display more elements on the screen than a small monitor. You can determine the size of a monitor by measuring diagonally from corner to corner. Keep in mind that if you see a computer ad that says "17-inch monitor (16.0-inch *viewable image size,* or v.i.s.)," this means that although the monitor has a full 17 inches of glass, only 16 inches of that glass are actually used to display the image.

Dot Pitch

To create an image onscreen, monitors activate small dots; these dots are phosphors on a CRT and liquid crystals on an LCD. The distance between each of these dots is called the *dot pitch*. This is a measure of the clarity of the monitor's image: The smaller the dot pitch, the sharper the image. Look for a monitor with a dot pitch of .26 millimeters (mm) or less.

Video Card

The *video card,* also known as the *graphics card,* is an internal circuit board that generates the images that you see on your monitor. Your main concern when purchasing a graphics card is the amount of *video memory* that it contains. With more video memory, you can set your computer display at a higher resolution, display more colors, and open many large graphics files at once.

Choose a Printer

A printer allows you to print out a document or photo from your computer. You can choose from a variety of printers with different capabilities to meet your printing requirements.

Printer Types

A *laser printer* uses a laser beam to etch text and images on the paper; lasers are fast and produce crisp images, but they tend to be expensive. An *inkjet* printer outputs text and images by spraying ink on the paper; an inkjet is slower and not as crisp as a laser printer, but it offers color output for far less money. A *photo printer* specializes in printing images from a digital camera.

Print Quality

Print quality, or *resolution,* is measured in *dots per inch* (dpi): The higher the quality, the sharper and more detailed the printed text or image. A typical laser printer has a print quality of 600 dpi, which means that each square inch of print has 600 dots across by 600 dots down (this is sometimes written as 600 x 600 dpi). For photo-quality inkjet output, look for a resolution of at least 2400 dpi.

Print Speed

Print speed is measured in *pages per minute* (PPM). A good laser printer for home or small office use can output pages at about 20 PPM. For inkjets and photo printers, a print speed of about 15 PPM is acceptable.

All-In-One Printers

For a slightly higher price than a standalone inkjet printer, you can get an all-in-one printer that also enables you to send and receive faxes, copy documents, and scan documents and photos. Keep in mind that the scanning and copying components have their own resolution values, with higher values giving you better-quality scans and copies.

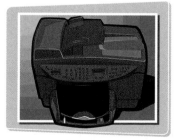

Add Other Peripherals

To complement your basic computer setup, you can add other hardware devices that expand the capabilities of your computer system.

Modem

If you want to establish a dial-up connection to the Internet, then you need to add a *modem* to your computer. A modem enables your computer to connect to the Internet through a telephone line. Look for a modem that supports 56 kilobits per second (Kbps), which is the connection speed supported by most Internet service providers.

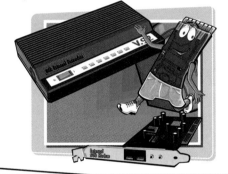

Audio Accessories

For you to hear the sounds generated by your computer, such as the music from audio CDs, your system needs a circuit board called a *sound card.* Most computers come with sound cards installed, although you can also upgrade to better sound cards that support Dolby digital sound and other audio features. You should also purchase separate speakers and, for the best audio experience, a subwoofer.

Network Card

A *network card* is a circuit board that enables your computer to join a network. You also need a network card if you want to surf the Internet using a high-speed connection. For more information about the Internet, see Chapter 9.

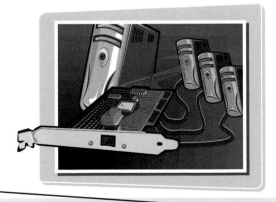

Wireless Accessories

If you want to join a wireless network with your notebook, tablet PC, or handheld PC, then you must ensure that your computer has wireless networking capabilities built in. This feature is usually designated as 802.11b or 802.11g. You also need a wireless router. For more information, see Chapter 12.

CHAPTER 3

Purchase Additional Software

Your computer's operating system comes with a number of programs. However, many of these programs have only minimal features, so you may want to upgrade to specialized applications.

Productivity Suite

A *productivity suite* (also called an *office suite*) is a collection of programs that usually includes a word processor, spreadsheet, presentation graphics program, and a database. The most popular, as well as the most expensive, is Microsoft Office. Less expensive alternatives are Microsoft Works and WordPerfect Office.

Graphics

If you want to create your own images, then you may want to use a different graphics program than the one that ships with your operating system. For example, you can choose graphics software such as Jasc Paint Shop Pro or Adobe Illustrator. If you want to work with digital photos, consider photo-editing programs such as Adobe Photoshop Elements and Microsoft Picture It!

Security

Although your operating system has limited built-in Internet security, you may want to upgrade to a more advanced security program. Some popular security programs are Norton Internet Security, ZoneAlarm Pro, and McAfee Internet Security Suite.

Educational

The personal computer is an excellent learning tool when you combine it with educational programs such as the Encarta Reference Library and Encyclopedia Britannica.

Tips on Purchase Considerations

Before you purchase a computer, you must consider other factors before making your decision.

Where to Buy

Always purchase your computer from a reputable store or online vendor, such as a well-known chain or smaller outlet that other people have recommended to you. Disreputable retailers abound in the computer business, and it is not worth taking a chance simply to save a few dollars.

Price

When buying your first computer, it is a good idea to avoid the low end and the high end of the price range. Low-priced computers are often too slow for day-to-day use and are made with cheap parts that may not last very long. High-priced computers are usually more powerful than what you need. Mid-priced computers generally have the best combination of quality and performance.

Promotions

You can often save money by watching for special promotions offered by computer dealers. For example, a dealer may offer extra RAM or an upgrade to a DVD burner free with the purchase of a new computer. Similarly, a retailer may include brand-name printers or other peripherals in the purchase at very low prices.

Expandability

To get the most out of your computer investment in the long term, you may want to expand the computer's capabilities rather than buy a completely new system. You should ensure that the computer has extra slots for memory modules, extra expansion slots for circuit boards, and spaces for extra CD-ROM or DVD drives. Avoid purchasing the smaller *mini-tower* cases, because they generally lack these expansion features. Instead, purchase a full-size tower case.

Installation

Many computer dealers offer to install your new system for a fee. However, it is easy to set up a basic computer system, so you may want to save your money and install the computer yourself. For more information about getting started with your computer, see Chapter 4.

Chapter 4

Getting Started with Your Computer

After you purchase your new computer, you need to set up and connect the components. If you are not already familiar with using a computer system, then you should also learn how to use basic devices such as the keyboard, mouse, and CD drive.

Set Up Your Work Area

To maximize your comfort and productivity, you should ensure that your desk and chair are adjusted properly. You should also ensure that the computer is located in a low-traffic area.

Sitting at the computer, typing, and using the mouse for long periods can cause injuries, including repetitive stress injuries (RSI) such as carpal tunnel syndrome. You can take steps to prevent these injuries.

Find a Good Place for Your Computer

Desk

Ensure that your computer desk is sturdy and stable. It should also have a large enough surface area to hold all of the computer's desktop components, as well as any books, papers, and other materials that you may use as you work.

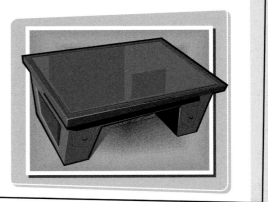

Chair

An uncomfortable or poorly designed chair can affect your work performance. You need a chair that has a contoured seat and good lower-back support. It should also have mechanisms to adjust the seat height as well as the angle of both the seat and the back support.

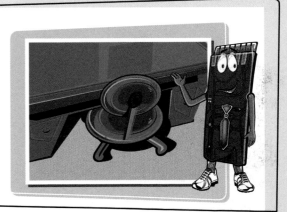

Location

Choose a location that is clean, dry, and cool. It should also be well lit, preferably from above or behind the monitor to prevent glare. Ensure that there is an electrical outlet nearby, as well as a telephone jack if you plan to use a modem. Avoid high traffic areas where people may bump into the computer case and possibly damage the system.

Position Components

A tower-style computer case goes on the floor, either under or beside the desk. The monitor, keyboard, and mouse sit on the desk. However, if you have a desktop-style computer case, then put the computer case on the desk and place the monitor on top of it. Speakers should also go on the desk, although if you have a subwoofer, you should place it on the floor for the best sound.

Basic Ergonomics

You can apply the principles of *ergonomics* to design a work area that maximizes your comfort and safety. Start with your chair. Sit up straight in your chair with your feet flat on the floor. Adjust the chair height so that your forearms are parallel to the floor when you type, and your eyes are level with the top of your monitor. You should also go for a walk at least once every hour.

Ergonomic Accessories

There are many accessories that you can buy to ensure good ergonomics. To help keep your wrists straight, you can use wrist rests on your keyboard and mouse. An adjustable keyboard tray helps to ensure that your keyboard is at the proper height. You can use a monitor stand to ensure that the monitor height is correct. To keep your feet flat, you can use a footrest.

Connect the Computer Components

On most PCs, the ports on the back of the case are color-coded to match the device plugs. In addition, most device plugs fit into only one type of port, so it is not possible to plug a device into the wrong port.

You can assemble your system by connecting the devices to the appropriate ports on the back of the computer case. If you are not comfortable assembling the system by yourself, ask a friend who is experienced with computers to help you.

Unpack the Components

Place the computer boxes on the floor and open them, preferably without using a knife. Remove each component and double-check with the packing list to ensure that you received everything that you ordered. If the computer arrived on a cold day, give the components a couple of hours to warm up to room temperature. At this stage, do not plug anything into an electrical outlet.

Connect the Monitor

Your monitor has two cables: a video cable and a power cord. The video cable has a D-shaped plug, which you can insert into the port with the same shape on the back of the PC. Leave the power cord unplugged for now.

Connect the Keyboard and Mouse

Plug the keyboard connector into the keyboard port, which is usually purple with a keyboard icon. Plug the mouse connector into the mouse port, which is usually green with a mouse icon.

Connect the Printer

The printer cable has a large connector for the printer and a slightly smaller connector, shaped like an elongated D, for the PC.

Connect the Modem

Run a telephone cable from your phone to the modem jack labeled *Phone*; run a second telephone cable from the wall jack to the modem jack labeled *Line* or *Telco*. If you have an external modem, then connect the serial cable to the PC's serial port.

Connect the Sound System

Connect one speaker to the PC's *Line Out* jack, and connect the second speaker to the first speaker. Connect your headphones to the *Headphones* jack. Connect your microphone to the *Mic* jack.

Connect USB Devices

If you have any USB devices, including your keyboard, mouse, or printer, connect them to your PC's USB ports.

Connect the Power Cord

You can now plug the power cords for all of your devices into your surge protector or power strip.

Turn On Your Computer for the First Time

Once you have connected your peripherals to your computer, you are ready to start your computer for the first time.

Turn On Your Peripherals

First, turn on all of your computer's peripheral devices. These include your surge protector or power strip, monitor, printer, and speakers.

Turn On Your Computer

Press your computer's power button, or flip its on/off switch. If you are using a notebook computer or tablet PC, you may need to hold down the power button for several seconds until the computer starts.

Troubleshoot Power-Up Problems

If nothing happens when you turn on your system, check the computer's power cord connections at both ends to ensure that you have properly plugged in the cord. Also, check that the surge protector or power strip is plugged in and turned on. Finally, ensure that you have turned on your monitor, and adjust the brightness control to a comfortable level.

Follow Setup Instructions

On Windows PCs, each manufacturer has its own setup program that runs the first time that you start the computer. This usually takes just a few minutes. You are typically asked for the following information:

• Your name and company name.

• A name for your computer.

• The username that you want to use when you log on to Windows.

Wait for the Operating System to Start

After the setup program ends, the operating system loads. The operating system will now load in this way each time that you turn on your computer. The startup is complete when you see the Windows desktop.

Use a Keyboard

The keyboard is your most important device for sending instructions and data to the computer, and so it is important to know how to use it.

Keep in mind that your keyboard layout may be different from the one shown here.

Shift

Hold down **Shift** and press a letter key to type the uppercase version of that letter. For example, if you hold down **Shift** and press **A**, the keyboard produces an uppercase "A".

Ctrl

You use **Ctrl** (pronounced control) in combination with other keys to run program features. For example, in most programs, if you hold down **Ctrl** and press **S** (written in this book as **Ctrl** + **S**), you save your current document.

Windows

Press the key to open the Windows operating system Start menu.

Alt

You use **Alt** in shortcut key combinations to run program features. For example, in most programs, if you hold down **Alt** and press **F4** (written in this book as **Alt** + **F4**), you close open programs.

Spacebar

Press the **Spacebar** to insert a space.

Specialty/Programmable Keys

Most new keyboards have keys for special tasks such as using the Internet or playing media. In many cases, you can also reprogram these keys to perform other functions.

Function Keys

The **F1** through **F12** keys are most often used as shortcut keys in programs. For example, in most programs, you can press **F1** to access the Help system.

Escape

Press **Esc** to stop the current task or when an application does something unexpected on your screen.

Caps Lock

Press to turn the Caps Lock feature on and off. The Caps Lock Status Light is illuminated when the Caps Lock feature is on. When Caps Lock is on, you can type all of your letters in uppercase. For example, when you press **A**, the keyboard produces an uppercase ìA". When Caps Lock is off, you type letters in lowercase. For example, when you press **A**, the keyboard produces a lowercase "a".

Application

In Windows, press the ▤ key to see the shortcut menu that is associated with the currently selected item on the screen.

Enter

In a text document, you can press `Enter` to start a new paragraph. In other contexts, you can press `Enter` to initiate or complete an action.

Backspace

Press the `Backspace` key to remove the character to the left of the cursor.

Delete

Press the `Delete` key to remove the character to the right of the cursor, or the character to the left of the cursor on a Mac keyboard.

Status Lights

When a status light is on, it tells you that the associated key is active. For example, if the Caps Lock light is on, the Caps Lock feature is activated.

Navigation Keys

Use the navigation keys to move through a document. Press `Home` to move to the beginning of the current line, or `End` to move to the end of the line. Press `Page Up` to move up one screen, or `Page Down` to move down one screen.

Arrow Keys

Use the arrow keys to move the cursor one character or one line at a time.

Num Lock

Press `Num Lock` to turn the numbers on the numeric keypad on or off. The Num Lock Status Light is illuminated when the Num Lock feature is on. When Num Lock is on, the keys on the numeric keypad produce numbers. When Num Lock is off, the keys on the numeric keypad become the keys indicated below the numbers.

Numeric Keypad

The numeric keypad allows you to quickly enter numbers when the Num Lock feature is on.

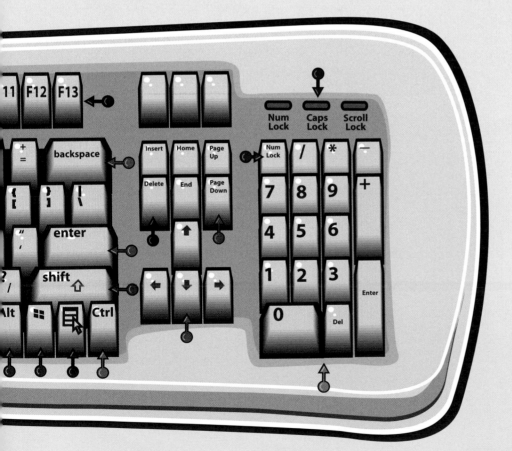

continued

Use a Keyboard

(continued)

Ergonomic

Ergonomic keyboards split the alphanumeric characters into two groups and angle those groups to the left and right. This allows you to position your hands more naturally when typing, which reduces wrist strain.

Notebook

Notebook computers are small, and so their keyboards tend to be cramped. This makes it harder to press the right keys, and therefore puts more strain on your wrists. In addition, most notebook keyboards have a key labeled Fn. This key appears in a different color, and you see characters in that same color on other keys. To access one of these characters, hold down `Fn` and press the key.

On-Screen

Tablet PCs have on-screen keyboards that you can use when the computer is in the tablet position that covers the physical keyboard. Use the digital pen to tap each character. Handheld computers that have no physical keyboard also use on-screen keyboards.

Add-On

If you do a lot of typing when using your handheld PC, the on-screen keyboard can become cumbersome. As an alternative, you can purchase an add-on keyboard that either attaches directly to the computer, or transmits your keystrokes wirelessly.

Keyboard Tips

Type Safely

Besides using an ergonomic keyboard, there are other techniques that you can use to avoid repetitive stress injuries caused by poor or extended typing. For example, you should position your hands properly on the keyboard by keeping your wrists flat while typing. You should position the keyboard so that your forearms are parallel to the ground. You should also shake your wrists often and take frequent breaks.

Do Not Spill Liquids

Liquids and keyboards do not go together. If you spill any liquid on your keyboard, then you may ruin it. This is particularly true of notebook keyboards, where spilling a liquid can damage the entire computer, usually beyond repair.

Learn to Type

If you have never typed before and plan to do a lot of typing, you can save a great deal of time by investing in a computer program that teaches you how to type.

Special Macintosh Keys

On a Mac keyboard, you use the Command (⌘) and Option keys in combination with other keys to run program features. For example, in most Mac programs, you press ⌘-S to save the current document. Similarly, you press Option-⌘-Esc to force a program to quit.

Use a Mouse

Today's computers are built with the mouse in mind, so it pays to learn the basic mouse techniques that you will use throughout your computing career.

If you have never used a mouse before, then you should remember to keep all your mouse movements slow and deliberate, while you are learning how to use it. You should also practice the techniques in this section as much as you can.

Mouse Techniques

CLICK THE MOUSE

❶ Position the mouse ⩤ over the object with which you want to work.

❷ Click the left mouse button.

● Depending on the object, the operating system either selects the object or performs some operation in response to the mouse click, such as displaying the Windows XP Start menu.

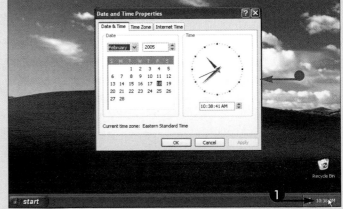

DOUBLE-CLICK THE MOUSE

❶ Position the mouse ⩤ over the object with which you want to work.

❷ Click the left mouse button twice in quick succession.

● The operating system usually performs some operation in response to the double-click action, such as displaying the Windows XP Date and Time Properties dialog box.

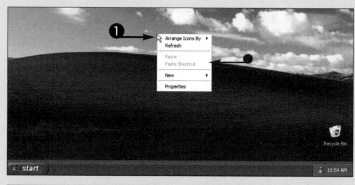

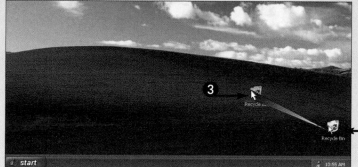

RIGHT-CLICK THE MOUSE

1 Position the mouse ⃗ over the object with which you want to work.

2 Click the right mouse button.

● The operating system displays a shortcut menu when you right-click an object.

Note: The contents of the shortcut menu depend on the object that you right-clicked.

CLICK AND DRAG THE MOUSE

1 Position the mouse ⃗ over the object with which you want to work.

2 Press and hold the left mouse button.

3 Move the mouse to drag the selected object.

In most cases, the object moves along with the mouse ⃗ .

4 Release the mouse button when the selected object is repositioned where you want it.

Why does Windows XP sometimes not recognize my double-clicks?
Try to double-click as quickly as you can, and be sure not to move the mouse between clicks. If you continue to have trouble, click **Start,** then click **Control Panel,** then click **Printers and Other Hardware,** and then click **Mouse**. In the Double-click speed group, click and drag the slider to the left, toward the Slow setting.

How can I set up my mouse for a left-hander?
Click **Start**, click **Control Panel**, then click **Printers and Other Hardware**, and then click **Mouse**. Click **Switch primary and secondary buttons** (☐ changes to ☑).

continued

Use a Mouse

(continued)

Two-Button Mouse

The standard mouse has a simple design with only two mouse buttons, although there are also three-button mice where you can program the middle button. The underside of the mouse contains a small ball that rotates when you move the mouse. The newer style of *optical mouse* uses an optical sensor instead of a ball.

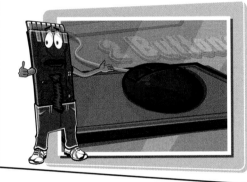

Wheel Mouse

A *wheel mouse* has a wheel between the two buttons. In many programs, when you rotate the wheel forward, the document scrolls up, and when you rotate the wheel backward, the document scrolls down.

Trackball

A *trackball mouse* is one in which the ball sits on top of the mouse. Instead of actually moving the mouse, you use your fingers or palm to rotate the ball while keeping the mouse stationary.

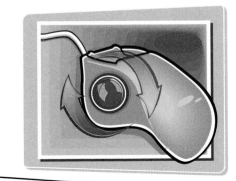

Touchpad

A *touch pad* is a flat, pressure-sensitive surface that is often used on notebooks or as a separate input device. You can move the mouse pointer by moving your finger along the surface of the pad. You click by tapping the surface with your finger, although most touch pads also include left and right buttons for clicking.

Pointing Stick

Resembling a pencil eraser, a *pointing stick* is a rubber cylinder that is used most often on notebook computers. You move the mouse pointer by nudging the pointing stick.

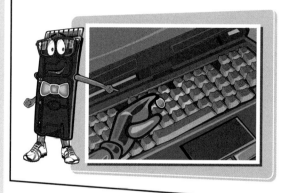

Digital Pen/Stylus

On a tablet PC, you can use the digital pen as a mouse. Hover the pen over the screen surface until you see the pointer, and then move the pen to move the pointer. Tap the screen surface to click. On a handheld PC, you can click by using the stylus to tap the screen.

Mouse Tips

Mouse Safety

Studies have shown that using the mouse excessively causes more repetitive stress injuries than excessive keyboarding. To prevent overuse injuries, keep your mouse at the same height as your keyboard, use a mouse wrist rest, and take frequent breaks. You can also learn program shortcut keys to reduce your mouse use.

Mouse Cleaning

If your mouse has a ball underneath, you should clean the ball periodically to ensure smooth operation. Turn the ball cover clockwise to release it, then remove and clean both the ball and the inside of the mouse.

Use a Floppy Disk Drive

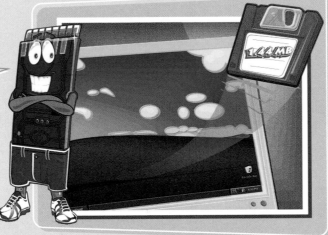

Today's computers, particularly Macintoshes and most notebooks, do not come with a floppy disk drive, so you may not have one on your computer.

You can use your computer's floppy disk drive to insert and read floppy disks. You can either open the files that are on the floppy disk, or store up to 1.44 MB of data on the disk.

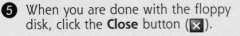

DISPLAY FLOPPY DISK CONTENTS

1 Insert the floppy disk in the floppy disk drive.

2 Click **start**.

3 Click **My Computer**.

The My Computer window appears.

4 Double-click 3½ **Floppy (A:)**.

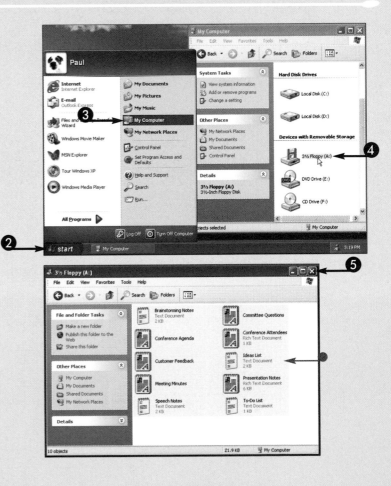

● The contents of the floppy disk appear.

5 When you are done with the floppy disk, click the **Close** button (☒).

The window closes.

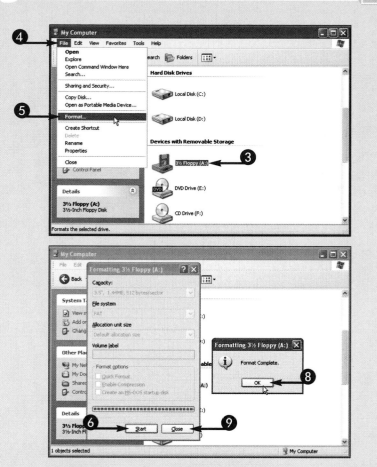

FORMAT A FLOPPY DISK

1 Insert the floppy disk in the floppy disk drive.

2 Follow Steps **2** to **3** on the previous page to display the My Computer window.

3 Click **3½ Floppy (A:)**.

4 Click **File**.

5 Click **Format**.

The Formatting 3½ Floppy (A:) dialog box appears.

6 Click **Start**.

Windows XP asks you to confirm the format operation.

7 Click **OK**.

Windows XP formats the disk and then displays a Format Complete message when it is done.

8 Click **OK**.

9 Click **Close**.

The dialog box closes.

How do I insert a floppy disk?
Hold the disk so that the metal sleeve is facing away from you and the writing on the sleeve is facing up. Insert the disk in the floppy disk drive slot until it clicks into place. To remove a floppy disk, press the eject button for the floppy disk drive and then slide out the disk.

How do I write-protect a floppy disk?
Each floppy disk has a locking mechanism that, when activated, prevents anyone from adding to, changing, or deleting the disk's contents. To lock a floppy disk, turn the disk over and look for the sliding tab that appears in one corner. Slide the tab toward the edge of the disk to lock it.

Use a CD or DVD Drive

You can use your computer's CD or DVD drive to insert a CD or DVD disc and access the files on the disc. If you have a recordable drive, you can burn your own files to a disc.

Most CD and DVD drives reside inside the computer case, but you can also add external drives to your computer.

Use a CD or DVD Drive

INSERT A CD OR DVD DISC

1 Press the button in the front of the drive.

The disc tray slides out.

2 Remove the disc from its case or sleeve.

Note: *When you handle the disc, be sure to touch only its edges.*

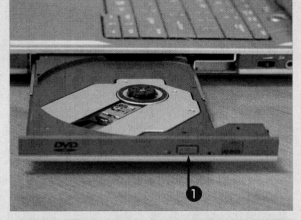
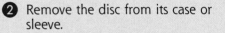

3 Place the disc, writing side up, in the drive's disc tray.

4 Press the drive button.

The disc tray closes.

Note: *In many cases, inserting a disc causes the operating system to automatically either display the contents of the disc or start the program contained on the disc. Therefore, you may not need to run through the steps on the next page.*

DISPLAY CD OR DVD CONTENTS

1. Insert the CD or DVD in the disc drive.

2. Click **start**.

3. Click **My Computer**.

   The My Computer window appears.

4. Double-click the CD icon or the DVD icon.

   ● The DVD icon.

   ● The CD icon.

   Note: *The name that appears beside the CD or DVD icon usually depends on the name given to the disc in each drive.*

   The contents of the disc appear.

5. When you are done with the CD or DVD, click ☒ to close the window.

   The window closes.

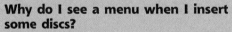

My drive does not have a disc tray. How do I insert the disc?
Some CD and DVD drives do not have disc trays. Instead, there is a narrow slot in the front of the drive. Insert your disc into that slot until it catches and inserts itself the rest of the way. Press the drive button to eject the disc.

Why do I see a menu when I insert some discs?
Windows XP recognizes certain types of discs, such as music CDs. After you insert the disc, you then see a menu of options that are appropriate to the type of disc. Click the option that you prefer, and then click **OK**.

Restart Your Computer

Knowing how to restart your computer is useful when you install a program or device that requires a restart to function properly. If you are busy, then you can always decide to restart your computer when it is more convenient.

You can restart your computer, so that it shuts down and starts up again immediately. This is useful if your computer is running slowly or behaving oddly. Sometimes a restart solves the problem.

Restart Your Computer

1 Shut down all of your running programs.

Note: Be sure to save your work as you close your programs.

2 Click **start**.

3 Click **Turn Off Computer**.

The Turn off computer window appears.

In Windows XP Professional, the Shut Down Windows dialog box appears.

4 Click **Restart**.

In Windows XP Professional, you can click 🔽, then click **Restart**, and then click **OK**.

Your computer shuts down and then restarts.

To restart a Macintosh computer, click the Apple menu (🍎) in the upper-left corner of the screen, then click **Restart**, and then click **Restart** again in the confirmation dialog box.

Turn Off
Your Computer

Shutting off the computer's power without properly exiting the operating system can cause two problems. First, if you have unsaved changes in some open documents, you will lose those changes. Second, you could damage one or more operating system files, which could make your computer unstable.

When you complete your work for the day, you should shut down your computer. However, you cannot just shut off the power. You must follow the proper steps to avoid damaging files on your system.

Turn Off Your Computer

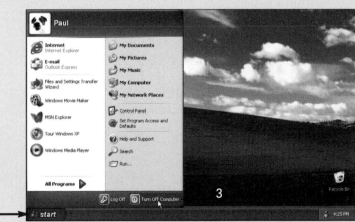

① Shut down all of your running programs.

Note: *Be sure to save your work as you close your programs.*

② Click **start**.

③ Click **Turn Off Computer**.

The Turn off computer window appears.

In Windows XP Professional, the Shut Down Windows dialog box appears.

④ Click **Turn Off**.

In Windows XP Professional, click ☑, then click **Shut down**, and then click **OK**.

Your computer shuts down.

To turn off a Macintosh computer, click the Apple menu (⌘) in the upper-left corner of the screen, then click **Shut Down**, and then click **Shut Down** again in the confirmation dialog box.

Chapter 5

Learning Windows XP Basics

Almost all new PCs have the Windows XP operating system installed. You can use Windows XP to start programs, manage files, connect to the Internet, and perform computer maintenance, and it is important to have a basic understanding of how Windows XP works.

Explore the Windows XP Screen

Before you can begin to understand how the Windows XP operating system works, you need to take a moment to become familiar with the basic screen elements.

Desktop
This is the Windows XP work area. It is where you work with your programs and documents.

Mouse Pointer
When you move your mouse, this pointer moves along with it.

Desktop Icon
An icon on the desktop represents a program or Windows XP feature. A program that you install often adds its own icon on the desktop.

Time
This is the current time on your computer. To see the current date, position the mouse pointer over the time. To change the date or time, double-click the time.

Notification Area
This area displays small icons that notify you about things that are happening on your computer. For example, notifications appear if your printer runs out of paper or if an update to Windows XP is available over the Internet.

Start Button
You can use this button to start programs and launch many of the Windows XP features.

Taskbar
The programs that you have open appear in the taskbar. You use this area to switch between programs if you have more than one running at a time.

Start a Program

To work with any program, you must first tell Windows XP which program you want to run. Windows XP then launches the program and displays it on the desktop.

Start a Program

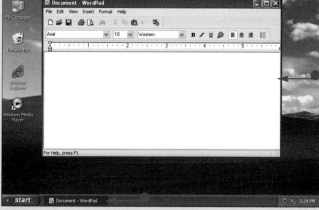

① Click **start**.

The Start menu appears.

If the program you want to launch appears on the Start menu, click the program and skip the rest of the steps in this section.

② Click **All Programs**.

The All Programs menu appears.

③ Click the submenu that contains your program.

④ Click the icon for the program that you want to launch.

● The program appears on the desktop.

● Windows XP adds a button for the program to the taskbar.

To shut down a program that you no longer need to use, click **File** and then click **Exit**, or press **Alt** + **F4**.

Switch Between Programs

If you are *multitasking* by running two or more programs at once in Windows XP, then you need to know how to switch from one program to another.

Switch Between Programs

1 Click the taskbar button of the program to which you want to switch.

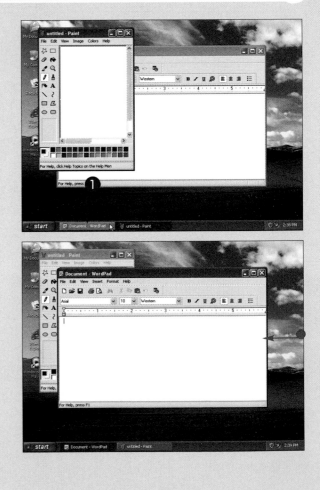

● Windows XP brings the program window to the foreground.

You can also switch to another window by clicking the window, even if it is in the background.

If you only have two programs open, you can switch between them from the keyboard by pressing **Alt** + **Tab**.

If you have more than two windows open, then hold down **Alt** and repeatedly press **Tab** until you get to the window in which you want to work.

Tour a Program Window

You can work with a program by accessing the various features in its window.

Minimize Button

Click the Minimize button (▬) to remove the window from the desktop and display only the windowís taskbar icon. The window is still open, but not active.

System Menu Icon

When you click this icon, you can work with program windows through the keyboard.

Title Bar

The title bar displays the name of the program. In some programs, the title bar also displays the name of the open document. To move the window, click and drag the title bar.

Menu Bar

The menu bar contains the drop-down menus for most Windows XP software.

Maximize Button

Click the Maximize button (▢) to enlarge the window so that it takes up the entire desktop.

Close Button

Click the Close button (✕) to exit the program.

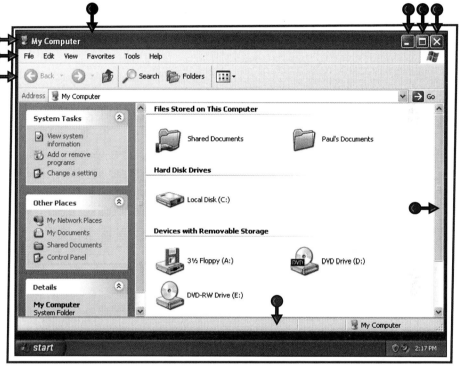

Toolbar

The toolbar contains buttons that offer easy access to common program commands and features. Some buttons are commands, while others display lists from which you can choose a command.

Status Bar

The status bar displays information about the current state of the program or document. For example, the status bar might tell you how many files you have selected or the number of the current page.

Scrollbar

Use the scrollbar to navigate a document. In a vertical scrollbar, click Scroll Up (▲) to navigate up, and click Scroll Down (▼) to navigate down. You can use a horizontal scrollbar to navigate left and right in a document.

Access a Command from a Drop-Down Menu

The items in a drop-down menu are either commands that run an action in the program or features that you turn on and off.

When you are working in a program, you can use the drop-down menus to access the program's commands and features.

Access a Command from a Drop-Down Menu

RUN COMMANDS

① Click the name of the menu that you want to display.

● The program displays the menu.

You can also display a menu by holding down **Alt** and pressing the underlined letter in the menu name.

② Click the command that you want to run.

The program runs the command.

If your command is in a submenu, click the submenu and then click the command you want.

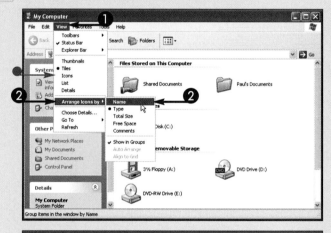

TURN FEATURES ON AND OFF

① Click the name of the menu that you want to display.

● The program displays the menu.

② Click the menu item.

You may have to click a submenu if your command is not on the main menu.

When you toggle a feature, the program turns the feature either on (☑) or off (no check mark appears).

For an option feature, the program turns on the item (◉) and turns off the previously activated item in the group.

Select a Command Using a Toolbar

Toolbars are collections of buttons that allow you to quickly access the program's most common features with a single click.

Most programs display one or more toolbars, usually at the top of the application window.

Select a Command Using a Toolbar

① Click the Toolbar button that represents the command or list that you want to access.

If the Toolbar button remains selected after you click it, this means that the button toggles a feature on or off, and that the feature is now on. To turn the feature off, click the button to deselect it.

● The program either runs the command or displays a drop-down list.

② Click the list item that represents the command.

The program runs the command.

DISPLAY AND HIDE TOOLBARS

① Click **View**.

② Click **Toolbars**.

③ Click the name of the toolbar that you want to display or hide.

If the toolbar is currently displayed in the Toolbars menu, the program hides the toolbar.

If the toolbar is currently hidden, the program displays the toolbar, and places a ☑ next to the toolbar name in the Toolbars menu.

Select Options from a Dialog Box

Dialog boxes appear when a program needs you to provide information. For example, when you access the options dialog box in a word-processing application, you can specify that different toolbars appear in the application window. You provide information by accessing various options and controls.

Dialog Box Controls

Tab
The various tabs in a dialog box display different sets of controls. You can choose from these settings to achieve a variety of results in Windows XP.

Option Button
You can click an option button to turn on a program feature. You can only select one option button in a group at a time. When you click an option button, it changes from ○ to ◉.

Check Box
You can click a check box to toggle a program feature on and off. If you are turning a feature on, the check box changes from ☐ to ☑. If you are turning a feature off, the check box changes from ☑ to ☐.

Combo Box
The combo box combines both a text box and a list box.

Drop-Down List Box
A drop-down list box displays only the selected item from a list. You can open the list and click to select a different item.

Spin Box
The spin box enables you to enter a numeric value.

Text Box
A text box allows you to type text.

List Box
A list box displays a list of choices from which you select the item you want. You may sometimes have to scroll through a list to find it.

Command Button
You can click a command button to run the command written on the button face. For example, you can click **OK** to apply settings that you choose in a dialog box, or you can click **Cancel** to close the dialog box without changing the settings.

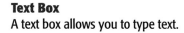

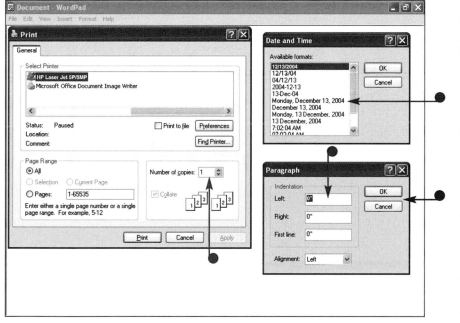

Use Dialog Box Controls

> You can use dialog boxes to control how a program works. Dialog boxes appear frequently, and allow you to specify settings for different features in the program.

For example, when you select the File menu's Print command to print a document, you can use the Print dialog box to specify the number of copies that you want to print.

Use Dialog Box Controls

TYPE TEXT IN A TEXT BOX

❶ Click inside the text box.

● A blinking, vertical bar called a *cursor* appears inside the text box.

❷ Press the **Backspace** or **Delete** keys to delete any existing characters.

❸ Type your text.

ENTER A VALUE WITH A SPIN BOX

❶ Click the top arrow on 🔼 to increase the value.

❷ Click the bottom arrow on 🔽 to decrease the value.

● You can also type the value in the text box.

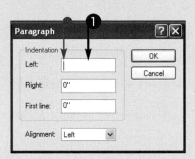

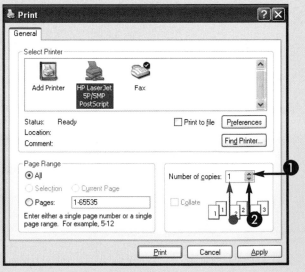

SELECT A LIST BOX ITEM

1 If necessary, click ☑ to scroll down the list and display the item that you want to select.

2 Click the item.

● You can click ☑ to scroll back up through the list.

SELECT AN ITEM FROM A COMBO BOX OR DROP-DOWN LIST BOX

● You can type the item name in the text box, or click the item in the list box to select it.

1 Click ☑.

● The list appears.

2 Click the item that you want to select.

Are there keyboard shortcuts that I can use to make it easier to work with dialog boxes?
Yes. Here are the most useful shortcuts:

Enter	Selects the default command button (which is indicated with a highlight around it).
Esc	Cancels the dialog box (which is the same as clicking Cancel).
Alt +letter	Selects the control that has the letter underlined.
Tab	Moves forward through the dialog box controls.
Shift + **Tab**	Moves backward through the dialog box controls.
↑ and **↓**	Moves up and down within the current option button group.
Alt + **↓**	Drops down the selected combo box or drop-down list box.

Save a Document

After you create a document and make any changes to it, you can save the document to preserve your work.

When you work on a document, Windows XP stores the changes in your computer's memory, which is erased each time you shut down your computer. Saving the document preserves your changes on your computers hard drive.

Save a Document

① Click **File**.

② Click **Save**.

In most programs, you can also press **Ctrl** + **S** or click **Save** ().

If you have saved the document previously, then your changes are now preserved, and you do not need to follow the rest of the steps in this section.

● If this is a new document that you have never saved before, then the Save As dialog box appears.

③ Click **My Documents**.

● If you want to save the document elsewhere, click ▼ in the **Save in** list, click the drive that contains the folder you want, and then double-click the name of the folder.

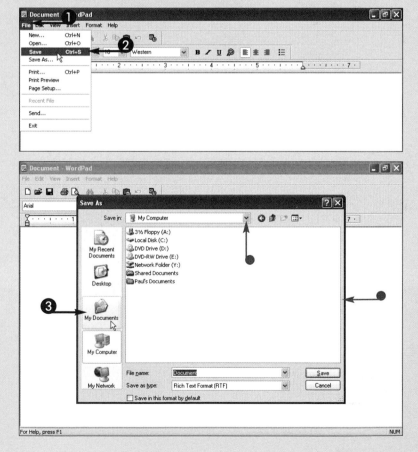

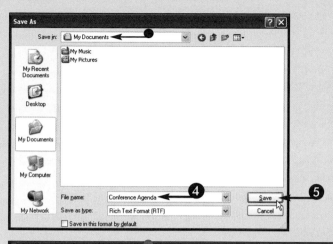

● Windows XP opens the My Documents folder.

④ Click in the **File name** field and type a name for the document.

You can type a name up to 255 characters long, but it cannot include the following characters: < > , ? : " \ *.

⑤ Click **Save**.

● The filename that you typed appears in the program's title bar.

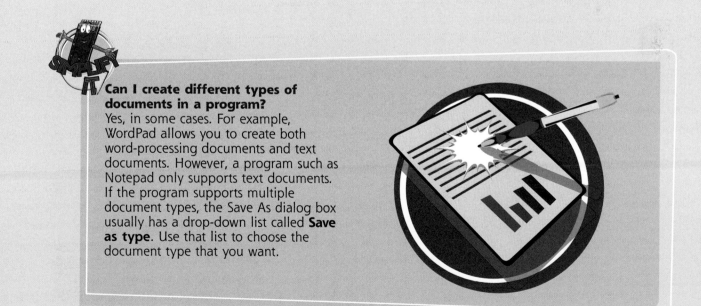

Can I create different types of documents in a program?
Yes, in some cases. For example, WordPad allows you to create both word-processing documents and text documents. However, a program such as Notepad only supports text documents. If the program supports multiple document types, the Save As dialog box usually has a drop-down list called **Save as type**. Use that list to choose the document type that you want.

Open a Document

To work with a document that you have saved in the past, you can open it in the program that you used to create it.

Open a Document

1. Start the program that you want to work with.

2. Click **File**.

   If you see a list of the most recently opened documents near the bottom of the File menu, and you see the document that you want, then click the name to open it. You can skip the rest of the steps.

3. Click **Open**.

   In most programs, you can also press **Ctrl** + **O** or click **Open** (📂).

4. Click **My Documents**.

   • If you want to open the document from another folder, click ☑ in the Look in list, then click the drive that contains the folder, and then double-click the name of the folder.

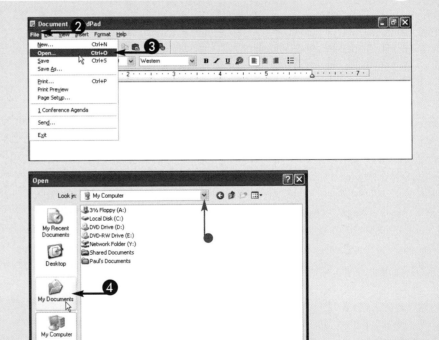

80

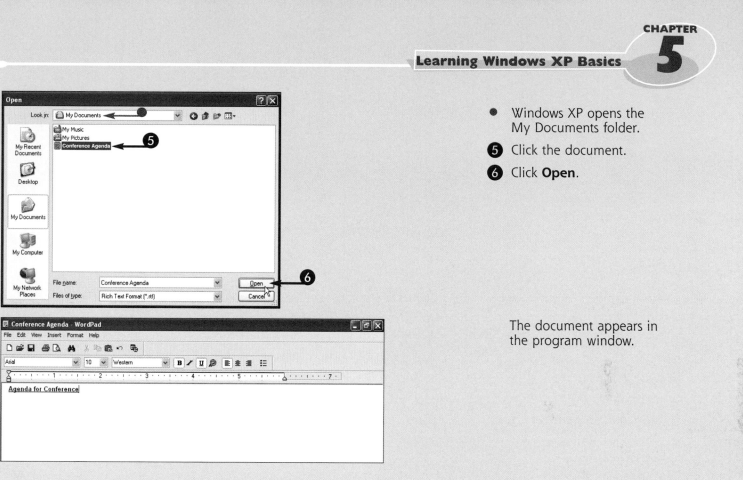

● Windows XP opens the My Documents folder.

⑤ Click the document.

⑥ Click **Open**.

The document appears in the program window.

Is there a more direct way to open a document?

Yes there is. You do not always need to open the program first. Instead, open the folder that contains the document and then double-click the document. Windows XP automatically launches the programs and opens the document.

① Click **start**.

② Click **My Documents**.

The My Documents folder appears.

③ Double-click the document.

Windows XP starts the program in which you created the document and then opens the document.

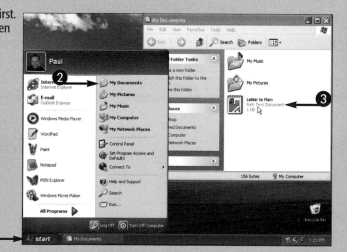

Print a Document

When you need a hard copy of your document, either for your files or to distribute to someone else, you can send the document to your printer.

Print a Document

① Turn on your printer.

② Open the document that you want to print.

③ Click **File**.

④ Click **Print**.

In many programs, you can select the Print command by pressing **Ctrl** + **P** or by clicking the **Print** button (🖨).

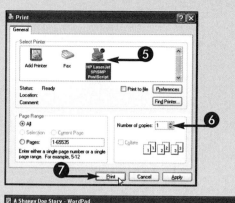

The Print dialog box appears.

The layout of the Print dialog box varies from program to program. The WordPad version shown here is a typical example.

5 If you have more than one printer, click the printer that you want to use.

6 Click the Number of copies 🔄 to specify the number of copies that you want to print.

7 Click **Print**.

In many programs, you can send a document directly to the printer by clicking 🖨.

● Windows XP prints the document. The print icon appears in the taskbar's notification area while the document prints.

How do I print only part of a document?
Most programs enable you to use the following methods to print only part of the document:

● Print selected text: Select the text that you want to print. In the Print dialog box, click the **Selection** option (○ changes to ◉) in the Page Range section.

● Print a specific page: Place the cursor on the page that you want to print. In the Print dialog box, click the **Current Page** option (○ changes to ◉) in the Page Range section.

● Print a range of pages: In the Print dialog box, click the **Pages** option (○ changes to ◉) in the Page Range section. In the text box, type the first page number, then a dash (−), and then the last page number (for example, 1-5).

Edit Document Text

> When you work with a character-based file, such as a text or word-processing document or an e-mail message, you need to know the basic techniques for editing, selecting, copying, and moving text.

Edit Document Text

DELETE CHARACTERS

① In a text document, click immediately to the left of the first character that you want to delete.

● The cursor appears before the character.

② Press ⟨Delete⟩ until you have deleted all the characters that you want.

An alternative method is to click immediately to the right of the last character that you want to delete and then to press ⟨Backspace⟩ until you have deleted all the characters you want.

If you make a mistake, immediately click **Edit,** and then click **Undo**. You can also press ⟨Ctrl⟩ + ⟨Z⟩ or click Undo (⟨↺⟩).

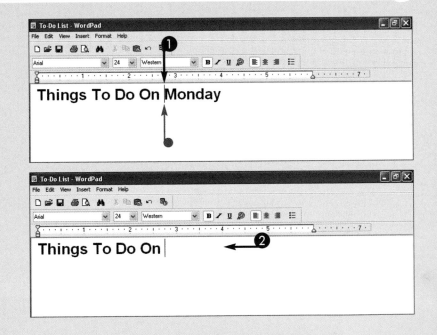

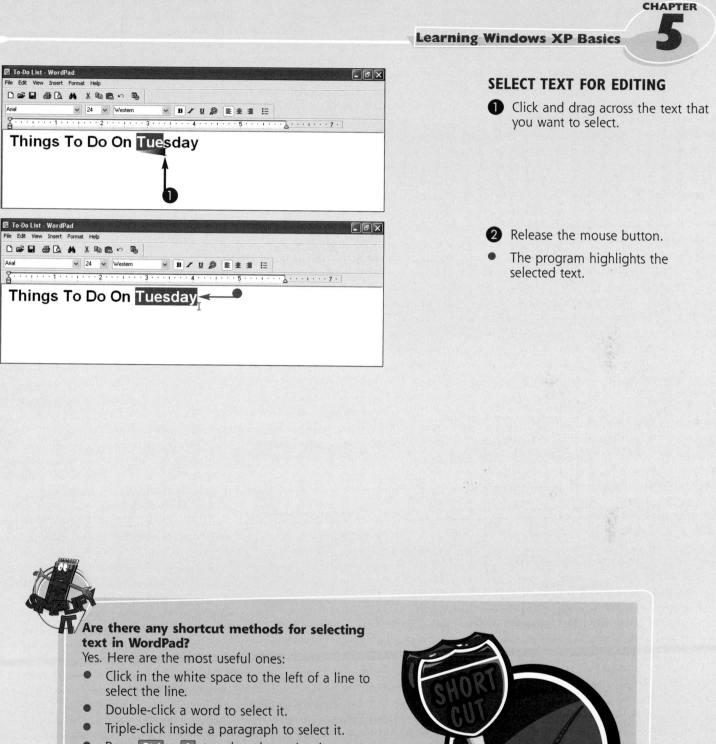

SELECT TEXT FOR EDITING

① Click and drag across the text that you want to select.

② Release the mouse button.

● The program highlights the selected text.

Are there any shortcut methods for selecting text in WordPad?

Yes. Here are the most useful ones:

● Click in the white space to the left of a line to select the line.

● Double-click a word to select it.

● Triple-click inside a paragraph to select it.

● Press Ctrl + A to select the entire document.

continued

Edit Document Text *(continued)*

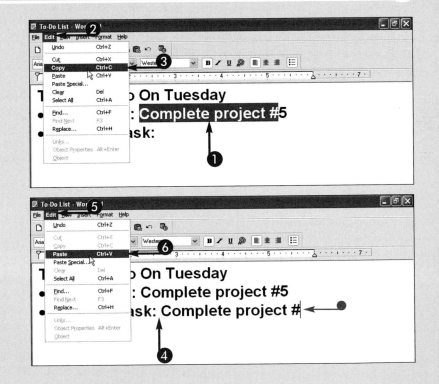

Once you select text, you can then copy or move the text to another location in your document.

COPY TEXT

① Select the text that you want to copy.

② Click **Edit**.

③ Click **Copy**.

In most programs, you can also press **Ctrl** + **C** or click **Copy** (📑).

④ Click inside the document at the position where you want the copy of the text to appear.

The cursor appears in the position where you clicked.

⑤ Click **Edit**.

⑥ Click **Paste**.

In most programs, you can also press **Ctrl** + **V** or click **Paste** (📑).

● The program inserts a copy of the selected text at the cursor position.

MOVE TEXT

① Select the text that you want to move.

② Click **Edit**.

③ Click **Cut**.

In most programs, you can also press **Ctrl** + **X** or click **Cut** (✂).

The program removes the text from the document.

④ Click inside the document at the position where you want to move the text.

The cursor appears at the position you clicked.

⑤ Click **Edit**.

⑥ Click **Paste**.

In most programs, you can also press **Ctrl** + **V** or click 📋.

● The program inserts the text at the cursor position.

How do I move and copy text with my mouse?

First, select the text that you want to move or copy. To move the selected text, place the mouse pointer over the selection and then click and drag the text to the new position within the document.

To copy the selected text, place the mouse pointer over the selection, hold down the **Ctrl** key, and then click and drag the text to the new position within the document.

Copy a File

You can make an exact copy of a file. This is useful when you want to make a backup of an important file on a floppy disk or other removable disk, or if you want to send the copy on a disk to another person.

You can copy either a single file or multiple files. You can also use this technique to copy a folder.

Copy a File

1 Locate the file that you want to copy.

2 Click the file.

To copy multiple files, click the first file that you want to copy, hold down **Ctrl** and then click each additional file that you want to copy.

3 Click **Edit**.

4 Click **Copy To Folder**.

The Copy Items dialog box appears.

5 Click the location where you want to store the copy.

If the folder where you want to store the copy is inside one of the displayed drives or folders, click ⊞ to navigate to the folder, and then click to select it.

6 Click **Copy**.

Windows XP places a copy of the file in the folder that you have selected.

Move a File

When you need to store a file in a new location, the easiest way is to move the file from its current folder to another folder on your computer.

You can use this technique to move a single file, multiple files, and even a folder.

Move a File

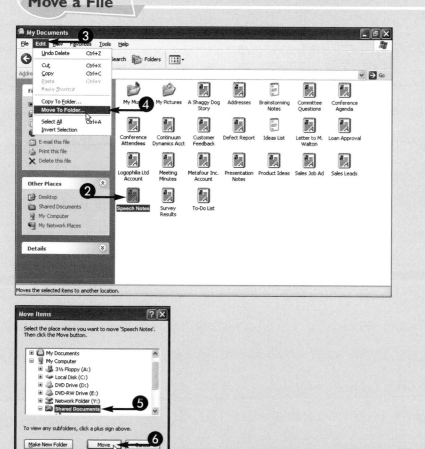

1 Locate the file that you want to move.

2 Click the file.

To move multiple files, click the first file that you want to move, then hold down **Ctrl** and click each additional file that you want to move.

3 Click **Edit**.

4 Click **Move To Folder**.

The Move Items dialog box appears.

5 Click the new location where you want to move the file.

If the folder where you want to move the file is inside one of the displayed drives or folders, click ⊞ to navigate to the folder, and then click to select it.

6 Click **Move**.

Rename a File

You should only rename those documents that you have created or that have been given to you by someone else. Do not rename any of the Windows XP system files or any files that are associated with your programs, or your computer may behave erratically, or even crash.

You can change the name of a file, which is useful if the current filename does not accurately describe the contents of the file. By giving your document a descriptive name, you make it easier to find the file later.

Rename a File

① Locate the file that you want to rename.

② Click the file.

You can also rename any folders that you have created.

③ Click **File**.

④ Click **Rename**.

A text box appears around the filename.

You can also select the Rename command by pressing F2.

⑤ Type the new name that you want to use for the file.

If you decide that you do not want to rename the file after all, you can press Esc to cancel the operation.

The name that you type can be up to 255 characters long, but it cannot include the following characters:
< > , ? : " \ *.

⑥ Press Enter or click an empty section of the folder.

The new name appears under the file icon.

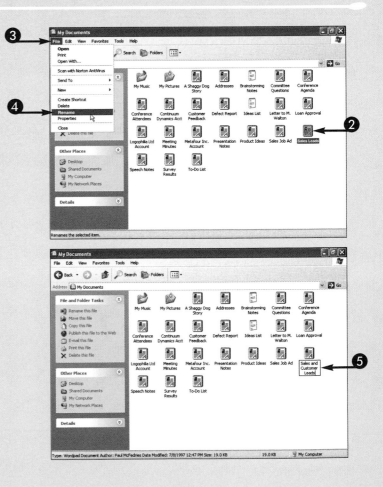

Delete a File

When you no longer need a file, then you can delete it. This helps you to prevent your hard drive from becoming cluttered with unnecessary files.

You should ensure that you only delete those documents that you have created or that have been given to you by someone else. Do not delete any of the Windows XP system files or any files that are associated with your programs, or your computer may behave erratically, or even crash.

Delete a File

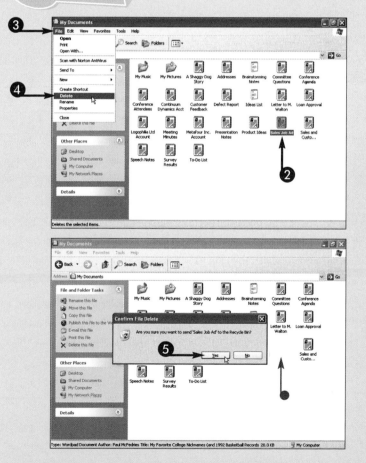

① Locate the file that you want to delete.

② Click the file.

To delete multiple files, click the first file that you want to delete, hold down `Ctrl` and click each additional file that you want to delete.

③ Click **File**.

④ Click **Delete**.

You can also select the Delete command when you press the `Delete` key.

The Confirm File Delete dialog box appears.

⑤ Click **Yes**.

● The file disappears from the folder.

You can also delete a file by clicking and dragging it to the desktop's Recycle Bin icon.

If you delete a file accidentally, you can restore it. Simply double-click the desktop's Recycle Bin icon to open the Recycle Bin window. Click the file, then click **File**, and then click **Restore**.

Chapter 6

Using Software

Software programs enable you to make your computer activities more practical and fun. For example, if you want to write a letter or a memo, you can use a word processor; if you want to create a newsletter or greeting card, you can use a desktop publishing program. This chapter shows you the basics of using software programs.

Create Documents with a Word Processor

Windows XP ships with a word processor called WordPad. OS X ships with the AppleWorks suite word processor. Other popular word processors include Microsoft Word, Corel WordPerfect, and Lotus Word Pro.

New High-Quality Document

You can use word-processing software to enable you to manipulate text and other elements to quickly create high-quality documents.

Format a Document

Apply a Typeface

A *typeface* — also called a *font* — is a distinctive character design that you can apply to the selected text in a document. Most word processors have a Font dialog box, which you can usually display by clicking **Format** and then **Font**. You can use the Font list to choose the typeface that you want.

Change Type Size

The *type size* refers to the height of each character, which is measured in *points*; 72 points equal one inch. In most word processors, you can change the size of the selected text, either by using the Font dialog box or by using the toolbar's Size drop-down list.

Format a Document

Apply Text Effects

Text effects are styles that change the appearance of the text. The most common examples are **bold**, *italics*, <u>underline</u>, and ~~strikethrough~~. In most word processors, you can apply effects either by using the Font dialog box or by using toolbar buttons. Some examples of buttons include bold ([**B**]), italic ([*I*]), underline ([<u>U</u>]), and strikethrough ([abc]).

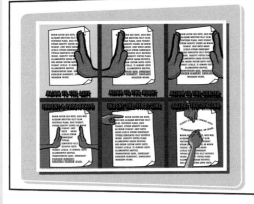

Format a Paragraph

One way to format a paragraph is to align text with the left or right margin, or to center it between the margins. Alternatively, you can indent a paragraph from the left or right margin, or you can indent just the first line. You can also adjust the spacing between lines within the paragraph and between paragraphs. In most programs, to access paragraph formatting, you can click **Format** and then click **Paragraph**.

Format a Page

Formatting the page usually involves three things: choosing the paper size, such as letter or legal; setting the margin sizes; and choosing the page orientation. Page orientations include portrait, where the text runs across the short side of the page, and landscape, where the text runs across the long side of the page. In most word processors, to format the page, you can click **File** and then click **Page Setup**.

continued

Create Documents with a Word Processor *(continued)*

Add Numbering or Bullets

Most word processors enable you to format a list of items in a way that is appropriate to the list's content. For example, if the list is a sequence of steps, you can format it as a numbered list. To start a numbered list in most programs, you can click ▤. However, if you have a nonsequential list of items, you can use a bulleted list. To start a bulleted list, you can click ▤.

Add Images

Word-processing documents are mostly text, but you can also insert images such as digital photos, clip art, scanned pictures, or artwork that you create. Images add variety and interest to a document and can complement the text by illustrating concepts or showing examples. Most word processors have an Insert menu that provides several commands for inserting images.

Find and Replace Text

All word processors have a Find feature that you access by clicking **Edit** and then **Find**. This feature enables you to search a document for a word or phrase. Word processors also come with a Replace feature that you can access by clicking **Edit** and then **Replace**. The Replace feature enables you to find specific text and then replace it with new text.

Choose Synonyms

The more powerful word processors come with a collection of writing tools that enable you to perfect your prose. One useful tool is the thesaurus in which you can enter a word and the program provides you with one or more synonyms. You can then pick the synonym that best conveys your meaning and use it in your document.

Check Spelling

Few things can mar your document as much as spelling mistakes. If other people read your documents, then you need a word processor that comes with a spell checker. This feature automatically checks each word for the proper spelling, suggests alternatives if it finds a mistake, and enables you to quickly fix the error.

Check Grammar

Grammar mistakes can be just as jarring as spelling mistakes, so a good word processor should check your grammar. This feature looks for errors such as in subject-verb agreement, capitalization, sentence fragments, and punctuation.

Crunch Numbers with a Spreadsheet

A spreadsheet is a software program that enables you to manipulate numbers and formulas to quickly create powerful mathematical, financial, and statistical models.

Although Windows XP does not come with a spreadsheet, the AppleWorks suite in OS X has a spreadsheet component. Other popular spreadsheet programs include Microsoft Excel, Corel Quattro Pro, and Lotus 1-2-3.

Spreadsheet Basics

Cell
A *cell* is a box in which you enter your spreadsheet data.

Column
A *column* is a vertical line of cells. Each column has a unique letter that identifies it. For example, the leftmost column is A, and the next column is B.

Row
A *row* is a horizontal line of cells. Each row has a unique number that identifies it. For example, the topmost row is 1, and the next row is 2.

Cell Address
Each cell has its own *address*, which is determined by the letter and number of the intersecting column and row. For example, the cell at the intersection of column C and row 10 has the address C10.

Range
A *range* is a rectangular grouping of two or more cells. The range address is given by the address of the top left cell and the address of the bottom right cell. I16:K21 is an example of a range of cells.

Build a Spreadsheet

Add Data

You can insert text, numbers, and other characters into any cell in the spreadsheet. Click the cell that you want to work with and then type your data in the formula bar. This is the large text box above the column letters. Your typing appears in the cell that you selected. When you are done, press Enter. To edit existing cell data, click the cell and then edit the text in the formula bar.

Add a Formula

A *formula* is a collection of numbers, cell addresses, and mathematical operators that performs a calculation. In most spreadsheets, you enter a formula in a cell by typing **=** and then the formula text. For example, the formula $=B1-B2$ subtracts the value in cell B2 from the value in cell B1.

Add a Function

A *function* is a predefined formula that performs a specific task. For example, the AVERAGE function calculates the average of a list of numbers, and the PMT function calculates a loan or mortgage payment. You can use functions on their own, preceded by = , or as part of a larger formula. Click 🔣 to see a list of the available functions.

continued

Crunch Numbers with a Spreadsheet *(continued)*

Calculate Totals Quickly

If you just need a quick sum of a list of numbers, click a cell below the numbers and then click the AutoSum button (Σ), which is available in most spreadsheets. In some spreadsheets, such as Excel, you can select the cells that you want to sum, and their total appears in the status bar.

Fill a Series

Most spreadsheet programs enable you to save time by completing a series of values automatically. For example, if you need to enter the numbers 1 to 100 in consecutive cells, you can enter just the first few numbers, select the cells, and then click and drag the lower-right corner to fill in the rest of the numbers. Most programs also fill in dates, as well as the names for weekdays and months.

Manage Lists

The row-and-column format of a spreadsheet makes the program suitable for simple databases called *lists*. Each column becomes a field in the database, and each row is a record. You can sort the records, filter the records to show only certain values, and add subtotals.

Enhance a Spreadsheet

Format Cells

All spreadsheet programs enable you to format cells and ranges to make your work more attractive and effective. You can format text with fonts, effects, sizes, and colors; add a border around a cell; change the background color of a cell; and align text.

Change Row and Column Sizes

The default column widths and row heights are not fixed. You can adjust the widths and heights to fit your cell data or to create special effects. To change the column width in most spreadsheets, you simply click and drag the right edge of the column header. To change the row height, you can click and drag the bottom edge of the row header.

Add a Chart

A *chart* is a graphic representation of spreadsheet data. As the data in the spreadsheet changes, the chart also changes to reflect the new numbers. Most spreadsheet programs support a wide variety of charts, including bar charts, line charts, and pie charts.

Build Presentations with a Presentation Program

Windows XP does not come with a presentation program, but the AppleWorks suite in OS X has a presentation component. Other popular presentation programs include Microsoft PowerPoint, Corel Presentations, and Lotus Freelance Graphics.

A presentation program enables you to build professional-looking slides that you can use to convey your ideas to other people.

Presentation Basics

Slide

A presentation consists of slides. Each *slide* is a single screen that can contain your text, images, and other data. A slide usually deals with only a single topic from your presentation, and you display just the topic basics — usually in point form — while you expand on the topic in your talk.

Slide Show

A *slide show* consists of a collection of slides in a presentation, as well as details such as the transitions between slides, slide animation effects, and narration. You can present the slide show on your computer, on the Internet, or on a CD-ROM, or project it onto a screen.

Build a Presentation

Add Content

Most slides consist of text, which usually consists of a slide title followed by several bulleted points. However, most presentation programs also enable you to enhance your slides with tables and nontext content such as charts, images, clip art, and even multimedia files such as sound clips and videos.

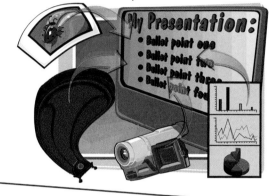

Add Animations and Transitions

You can change how the slide content appears by using animation. For example, you can set up the slide to show only one bullet at a time. You can also change the transition from one slide to another. For example, you can fade the current slide out and into the next slide.

Format the Slides

All presentation programs enable you to format your slides for maximum readability and impact. You can format text with fonts, effects, sizes, and colors; change the paragraph spacing and text alignment; and add a background color or image.

Run the Slide Show

Most presentation programs give you a great deal of flexibility for setting up the slide show. For example, you can choose to advance the slides manually by clicking the mouse, or automatically at a defined interval. You can loop the slides, and turn narration on and off.

Manipulate Pictures with an Image Editor

Windows XP ships with a drawing program called Paint, whereas the AppleWorks suite in OS X has both drawing and painting components. Other popular image editors include Adobe Photoshop, Jasc Paint Shop Pro, and CorelDRAW.

An image editor enables you to create, view, and manipulate pictures, drawings, digital photos, scanned images, and other types of graphic files.

Obtain Images

Create Images

Drawing and painting programs enable you to create your own images. You can use a drawing program for relatively simple line drawings, whereas you can use a painting program for more elaborate works. Both types of programs offer a number of tools for creating shapes, drawing freehand, and applying colors.

Import Images

All image editors enable you to open existing image files that are stored on your computer. If the image you want is stored on a digital camera or exists on paper, most image editors can acquire the image from the camera or a document scanner.

Work with Images

Manipulate Images

Once you open the image in an image editor, the program offers a number of methods for manipulating the image. For example, you can change the size, crop out parts that you do not need, and flip or rotate the image.

Enhance Photos

The better image editors include a number of tools that enable you to retouch and enhance your photos. For example, you can remove red-eye, adjust the color balance and contrast, and sharpen the image.

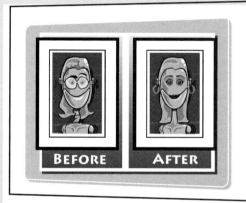

BEFORE   AFTER

Add Effects

Most image editors also enable you to add special effects to an image. For example, you can make a photo look like it was drawn with charcoal or pencil, distort the image, and add textures.

Create Publications with a Desktop Publishing Program

A desktop publishing program enables you to compose professional-looking publications that combine text and images. For example, you can create flyers, brochures, greeting cards, catalogs, newsletters, and letterheads.

Popular desktop publishers include Microsoft Publisher, Adobe PageMaker, and QuarkXPress.

Get Started

Choose a Publication Type

Your first step with a desktop publishing program is to choose the type of publication that you want to compose. Most desktop publishing programs offer a number of publication types. These types add a number of design elements automatically, which is easier than creating the entire document yourself.

Choose a Design

Once you have chosen your publication type, your next step is to choose an overall design for the publication, which includes text formatting, page layout, and graphic accent elements. This saves you from having to construct these items yourself.

Add Content

Add or Edit Text

Prefabricated publications contain text placeholders that say things like "Name of Recipient" and "Business Name." Click these placeholders and type the text that you want. To add new text, you insert a text box and type your text in the box.

Add Images

All desktop publishing programs enable you to add image files to your publication, either as new images or as replacements for images in the prefabricated designs.

Lay Out the Page

Click and Drag

Once all of your publication elements are on the page, you then need to adjust the page layout to maximize the attractiveness and effectiveness of the publication. Each text box and image on the page is a separate item that you can click and drag with your mouse to move to the appropriate location.

Arrange Objects

All desktop publishing programs allow you a number of options for arranging the page elements relative to the page or to each other. For example, if two images overlap, you can send one image behind the other. You can also align objects with each other, and wrap text around images.

Chapter 7

Using Multimedia

You can use a combination of software and hardware to play, view, and edit a wide variety of multimedia. For example, you can use your computer to listen to sounds and music, and view photos, drawings, videos, and animations.

How a Digital Camera Works

You can use a *digital* camera to take photos that the camera stores *internally* on a *memory card*. You can then connect the camera to your computer and transfer some or all of the photos to your hard drive.

Megapixels

One of the most important features of a digital camera is the number of megapixels, which measures the detail in each photo. A megapixel represents a million pixels. See the section "Discover Digital Images" to learn more about pixels.

The number of megapixels affects the quality of the image; the more megapixels, the better the picture. A low-end camera may take photos that are 2 or 3 megapixels, whereas better cameras take photos that are 7 or 8 megapixels or more.

Memory

All digital cameras have some form of internal memory — usually in the form of a memory card, such as a CompactFlash card — that they use to store the photos that you take. If you take a photo that you do not like, you can delete it from memory and try again.

The amount of memory affects the number of photos that the camera can store internally, so the more memory the camera has, the more photos it can store.

Features

Today's digital cameras come with many of the features that are found in film cameras, including built-in flashes and zoom lenses. Some digital cameras also come with LCD screens and are able to capture short video sequences.

Transfer Photos

When you are ready to work with your photos, connect your digital camera to your computer. Most digital cameras connect through a USB cable. Then use the software that came with the camera to transfer the images to your computer. When the transfer is complete, delete the images from the camera so that you can store new photos.

How a Digital Video Camera Works

You can use a *digital video camera* to record *videos* that the camera stores internally. You can then connect the *video camera* to your computer and transfer the *video* to your computer for editing.

Megapixels

Similar to a digital still camera, the quality of the digital video camera image is also rated by the number of megapixels it supports. Digital video cameras use an internal chip called a Charged Coupling Device (CCD) to capture video, and different CCDs support different levels of detail.

Most current digital video cameras come with CCDs that support between 1 and 3 megapixels. Some older or low-end digital video cameras use CCDs that only support about 700,000 pixels.

Storage

Digital video cameras store your video footage internally until you are ready to transfer the footage to your computer. Digital video cameras use a wide variety of storage devices, from MiniDV cassette tapes, to memory cards such as MultiMedia and Secure Digital, to recordable DVD discs. If you capture footage that you do not like, you can erase it and try again.

Most MiniDV tapes hold between 60 and 120 minutes of video, and recordable DVDs hold between 30 and 120 minutes. For cameras that use memory cards, the more memory the camera has, the more video it can store.

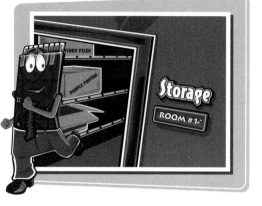

Features

Most digital video cameras come with an LCD monitor and zoom controls, and some have the ability to take still pictures. Most digital video cameras can capture footage at 30 frames per second (fps), which produces smooth motion. However, some cameras can only record 320-x-240-pixel videos at 30 fps; at the regular size, 640-x-480-pixel video, they can only capture 15 fps.

Transfer Videos

When you are ready to work with your videos, you can connect your digital video camera to your computer. Most digital video cameras connect to the computer using a USB cable, although some cameras use a FireWire cable (also called IEEE 1394 or iLink). You can then use the software that came with the camera to transfer the video footage to your computer. When the transfer is complete, either insert a new tape, card, or disc, or delete the footage from the camera, so that you can store new videos.

How a Web Cam Works

You can also use a Web cam to record live video for use in video conversations or video e-mail.

You can use a *Web cam*, also called a *PC cam*, to capture live photos directly to your computer or to an Internet site.

Live Photos

Most Web cams come with special software that enables you to capture live photos at regular intervals. You can then send each new photo to your Web site to create a constantly updated view of a scene or object. Most Web-cam software also enables you to send a photo through e-mail.

Live Video

Many Web cams can also capture live video directly to your computer, which is useful for Internet-based video conversations or videoconferencing. For most Web cams, you face a trade-off between the size of the video and number of frames captured per second. For example, a Web cam may capture a 352-x-288-pixel video at 30 frames per second, or a 640-x-480-pixel video at 15 frames per second.

Video Conversation

A *video conversation* — or *video chat* — is an Internet-based form of communication in which two people can both see and hear each other. To have a video conversation, both parties need a Web cam, a sound card, speakers, a microphone (note that many Web cams have built-in microphones), and software such as Windows Messenger or OS X iChat. For more information, see Chapter 11.

Video E-Mail

A *video e-mail* is an e-mail message that includes a video captured by a Web cam as an attachment. Most Web-cam software programs enable you to capture the live video stream, compress it, and then attach it to an e-mail. Video e-mail is a convenient way to pass along short home movies to friends or family who do not have a Web cam of their own.

Site Monitoring

A Web cam is a useful tool for monitoring a site. For example, you could enhance the security of your home or office by using a Web cam to monitor a live feed of a secure area. Similarly, many parents use Web cams to monitor toddlers and children. Some Web cams have built-in motion sensors so that they transmit video only when they detect movement.

How a Digital Audio Player Works

You can use a *digital* audio *player,* also called an *MP3 player,* to store and *play digital* music *files. Digital* audio *players* are *small, lightweight,* and *sturdy,* so you can *listen* to music *while walking, jogging,* or *performing* errands.

Some popular digital audio players include the Apple iPod, the iRiver IFP series, the Rio Carbon, and the Creative Labs MuVo.

Storage

Most digital audio players store music files internally using *flash memory*, memory chips that allow for quick recording and erasing of files. The flash memory is built either into the player or on removable memory cards, such as CompactFlash cards. 512MB of flash memory is enough to store about 8 hours of music.

Some players, such as the Apple iPod and the iRiver H340, have internal hard drives that can store anywhere from 1GB to 40GB of music, or between 16 and 640 hours of music. Most players support at least two music file formats: MP3 and WMA. For more about these file types, see "Understanding Digital Audio."

Features

Digital audio players range from simple devices that only play music to more complex machines that offer a number of extra features. For example, many players have FM tuners that enable you to listen to FM radio. Other players have built-in microphones for voice recording. For walking or jogging with your player, you might need either an arm strap or a belt clip.

Access Music

Most digital audio players connect to the computer through a USB cable. The players also use software that enables you to organize your music files and send them to the player. Your operating system also has built-in software that allows you to organize and play music files: Windows XP has Windows Media Player, and OS X has iTunes.

The simplest way to get music onto your digital audio player is to first transfer one or more tracks from an audio CD to your computer. You can then upload those tracks to your player. Alternatively, go to an Internet site that offers digital music files, such as MP3.com or Apple's iTunes Music Store.

Discover Digital Images

A digital image is any picture that exists in an electronic format, including photos, drawings, scanned pictures, and clip art. Once you have digital images on your computer, you can incorporate them into presentations, reports, e-mail messages, and Web pages.

PHOTO OF JAKE

SUNSET OVER MOUNTAINS

A BEAUTIFUL FLOWER

Understanding digital images requires that you learn about a few fundamental concepts, such as pixels, image resolution, color quality, image compression, and file formats.

Pixels

A *pixel* — short for *picture element* — is a tiny square of light on your screen. Everything you see on your computer is displayed by changing the colors of individual pixels. A typical screen can have anywhere from 480,000 to nearly 2 million pixels, arranged in a row-and-column grid.

Resolution

The image *resolution* is given by the density of the pixels in the image. The higher the resolution — that is, the higher the pixel density — the sharper the image. Image resolution is measured in *pixels per inch,* or PPI. Typical values are 75, 150, and 300 PPI.

300-PPI

75-PPI

Color Quality

The *color quality* — also called the *bit depth* — is the number of possible colors used in an image. The higher the color quality, the sharper your images appear. Common color quality values are 256 colors (also called 8-bit color), 65,536 colors (16-bit), and 16 million colors (24-bit).

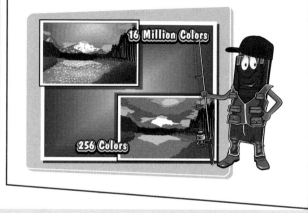

Work with Images

You can use image-editing software to view and edit your digital images. For example, you can change the image size, crop out elements that you do not want, or add special effects. You can print the photos on a color or photo printer, or you can have a photo store print them for you.

Image Compression

To make large digital files easier to manipulate, most images are compressed to a certain extent to make them smaller. Some formats use *lossy compression*, which removes portions of the image that are redundant or unneeded. Other formats use *lossless compression*, which maintains the integrity of the original image. In general, lossy compression generates files that are smaller but of poorer quality than files generated by lossless compression.

File Formats

You can save digital image files in a variety of formats, each of which has its own features and advantages. For example, BMP (bitmap) images use lossless compression and are good for color drawings. JPEG images use lossy compression, and the resulting small files are good for uploading to a Web site or sending through e-mail. TIFF images use lossless compression and are good for rendering photos and scanned images.

Learn About Digital Video

A digital video is a series of consecutive pictures that produce a moving image that exists in an electronic format. This includes files transferred from a digital video camera, live feeds from a Web cam, DVD movies, and animations. Once you have digital videos on your computer, you can incorporate them into presentations, e-mail messages, and Web pages.

Understanding digital videos requires that you learn about a few fundamental concepts, such as frame rates, video size, video compression, and video file formats.

Frame Rate

The *frame rate* measures the number of still images, or *frames,* that a digital video file displays every second. The frame rate is measured in *frames per second* (fps). The higher the frame rate, the smoother the motion appears in the digital video; however, this results in a larger file and the need for more processing power. The two most common frame rates for digital video are 30 fps (*full-motion video),* which produces smooth motion, and 15 fps, which produces jerky motion.

Video Size

The *video size* measures the dimensions — the width and height — of the video frames, expressed in pixels. For example, a 320 x 240 video has frames that are 320 pixels in width and 240 pixels in height. The greater the video size, the larger the file size, and the more processing power that is required to play the file. The most common digital video sizes are 320 x 240, 640 x 480, and 720 x 480 (also called *full-screen video).*

Work with Videos

After you transfer the video to your computer, you can use video-editing software to view and edit the video. Windows XP offers Windows Movie Maker, whereas OS X offers iMovie. There are also third-party products such as Adobe Premier and Roxio VideoWave. You can rearrange clips, add sound effects, and insert transitions between scenes.

Video Compression

Digital video files can be huge, so some compression is required to make the files easier to work with. All video compression formats use *lossy compression*, which removes portions of the video that are redundant or unneeded. For example, the compression may record only the data that changes from one frame to another, rather than entire frames.

File Formats

You can save digital video files in a variety of formats, each of which has its own features and advantages. The most common format is MPEG (Motion Picture Experts Group), which uses lossy compression and has three main standards: MPEG-1 produces near-VHS quality video; MPEG-2 produces DVD-quality video; and MPEG-4 is an enhanced version of MPEG-2 that produces even smaller files.

WMV (Windows Media Video) is similar to MPEG-4, but produces even smaller files. AVI files are limited to 320 x 240 pixels at 30 fps, but are supported by all versions of Windows. You can play QuickTime files on both Mac and Windows computers.

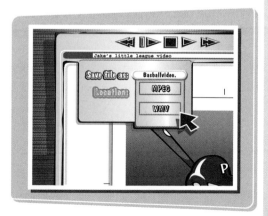

Understanding Digital Audio

Understanding digital audio requires that you learn about a few fundamental concepts, such as digital sampling, bit rates, MP3s and other audio file formats, and music licensing.

Digital audio is any sequence of sounds that exists in electronic format, including music, audio CDs, sound effects, recorded sounds, and the narration or soundtrack that accompanies a digital video. Once you have digital audio on your computer, you can listen to it as well as incorporate it into presentations, digital video projects, and Web pages.

Digital Sampling

Digital sampling is the process by which an analog sound wave is converted into a digital format. A sample is a snapshot of the sound wave at a given moment. The sample is a measurement of the wave's height (its loudness or *amplitude*), and these measurements are taken at discrete intervals to form a digital approximation of the original wave.

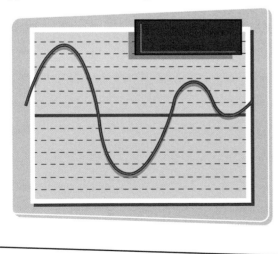

Bit Rate

The *bit rate* — also spelled *bitrate* — measures the digital sampling rate that is used to create a digital audio file. Bit rate is measured in *thousands of bits per second* (Kbps). Although a higher bit rate results in a better sound quality, it also results in a larger file. For example, a digital audio file sampled at 128 Kbps (called *near-CD quality*) sounds better than one that is sampled at 64 Kbps (called *FM radio quality*), but the resulting file is twice as large.

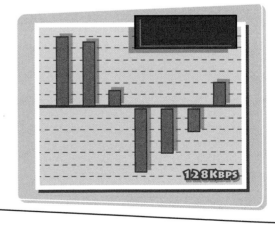

MP3s

The Motion Picture Experts Groups Audio Level 3, or MP3, is one of the most popular audio file formats. It compresses digital audio by removing extraneous sounds that are not normally detected by the human ear. This results in high-quality audio files that are one-tenth the size of uncompressed audio, thus making MP3s ideal for downloading and storing on digital audio players (which are frequently called *MP3 players*, even when they support other audio formats).

Other File Formats

Besides MP3, digital audio comes in a number of other file formats. The most popular of these is Windows Media Audio (WMA), which produces audio files with the same quality as MP3, but that are compressed to about half the size. WMA is often used for digital audio player storage because it can fit twice the number of songs as MP3. The WAV format is supported by all Windows versions, but it is uncompressed and so is suitable for only short sound effects or snippets. Less popular audio formats are MIDI, AIFF, and AU.

Work with Digital Audio

You can use audio-editing software to play and edit your digital audio. For example, you can delete portions of the file, change the volume or speed, and add special effects. You can also use some audio-editing programs to record sounds through a microphone or from an external audio source such as a turntable, cassette player, or digital audio tape player.

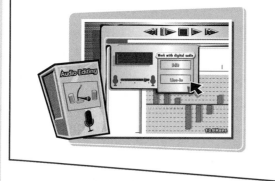

Digital Audio Licenses

Some digital audio content is in the public domain, which means that you can use it without paying for it. However, most digital audio content — particularly commercial music — is protected by copyright. This means that legally you should not play the audio unless you get permission or pay a fee. In either case, you are given a digital license that allows you to play the audio file, and that may also place restrictions on whether you can copy the file to devices other than your computer.

Chapter 8

Working with Portable Computers

Whether you are looking to purchase a portable computer or you are trying to get the most out of your existing portable computer, the information in this chapter will help you.

Advantages of a Portable Computer

Most portable computers are as powerful as a desktop computer, but they are also lightweight and small enough to take with you when you leave your office or home.

Lightweight

Portable computers are designed to be light enough to take with you wherever you go. Notebooks, also called *laptops*, generally weigh around 5 or 6 pounds. Handheld PCs, also called *palmtops*, generally weigh just a few ounces.

Powerful

Depending on the configuration, notebook computers can be just as powerful as desktop systems. A notebook with a fast processor, a copious amount of memory, and a large hard disk can do anything that the equivalent desktop system can do.

Cable-Free

Portable computers come with the keyboard, mouse, and display packaged into a single, self-contained unit. This makes portable computers easy to set up and use because, for basic operations, you do not need to connect anything to the computer.

Battery Operation

Desktop systems require an AC outlet. Portable computers, on the other hand, can run off their internal batteries if AC power is not available. This enables you to use a portable computer almost anywhere, including a coffee shop, taxi, airplane, and even a park.

Upgradeable

Notebook computers are self-contained units, but most of them are also upgradeable through PC Cards that enable you to augment your computer with a modem, network card, hard drive, and many other devices.

Presentations

The bright, flat notebook screen is excellent for displaying presentations and similar visual material. As a result, you can take your notebook computer to a meeting and use it to present information.

Learn About the Portable Computer Battery

A portable computer has an internal battery that enables you to operate the computer without the use of an electrical outlet. The battery also serves as a backup source of power should the electricity fail.

Battery Types

Nickel Metal Hydride Battery

Older portable computers use rechargeable nickel metal hydride (NiMH) batteries. The NiMH type is being phased out because it can suffer from a problem called the *memory effect*, where the battery loses capacity if you repeatedly recharge it without first fully discharging it.

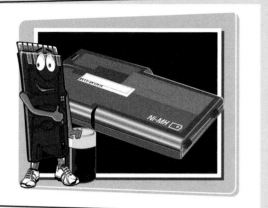

Lithium-ion Battery

Almost all new notebooks have rechargeable lithium-ion (Li-ion) batteries. Li-ion batteries are lighter and last longer than NiMH batteries, and Li-ion batteries do not suffer from the memory effect.

Bridge Battery

Some portable computers have an internal *bridge battery* — also called a *RAM battery* — which is designed to maintain power to the computer's memory in the event that your main battery shuts down. This enables you to avoid losing your work while you plug the computer into an electrical outlet.

Battery Cycling

Cycling a battery means letting it completely discharge and then fully recharging it again. To maintain optimal performance, you should cycle your portable computer battery if you have not used the battery for several months.

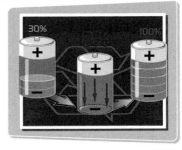

Extra Battery

If you think you will be without electrical power for an extended period, consider purchasing an extra battery, and be sure to fully charge both batteries before you leave. When the charge on the first battery is low, shut down your portable computer, swap the used battery with the fresh one, and then restart your computer. If your computer has a bridge battery, you can change the batteries without shutting down.

Limited Battery Life

The battery enables you to operate the notebook for only short periods, usually no more than a few hours. To avoid losing work, you should monitor the battery so that it does not run out of power. This information can also help you to extend battery power by shutting down components when you are not using them.

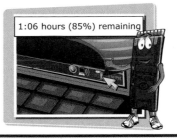

Windows XP

In Windows XP, use the Power Meter icon in the taskbar's notification area. When the battery is at maximum charge, the icon appears all blue (). As the battery charge decreases, the amount of blue in the icon also decreases. For example, when the battery is at 50% charge, the icon appears half blue ().

OS X

To monitor your iBook or PowerBook battery in OS X, click the Battery Meter icon (). OS X displays the remaining battery time.

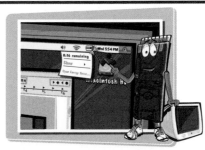

Maximize Battery Power

When running your portable computer on its batteries, maximizing the battery power is crucial. You need to treat your battery with care and take advantage of the power management features of your operating system.

Note that running a portable computer on batteries is always a trade-off between battery life and computer performance. The more diligent you are about preserving battery life, the slower your computer will operate.

General Tips

Fully Charge New Batteries

When you get a new portable computer or a new replacement battery, the battery usually comes fully discharged. Be sure to fully charge the battery before you use it for the first time. In addition, you should cycle the battery the first two or three times that you use it.

Exercise Batteries

To maintain effectiveness, you need to use your battery often. Even if you always run your portable computer on electrical power, you should switch to battery power at least once a month.

Use Sleep Modes

You can save power by choosing to send your computer into either standby or hibernate mode. *Standby* means that the computer components are temporarily turned off. *Hibernate* means that the entire computer is shut down, although Windows XP saves all of your open windows.

Specify a Power Scheme

You can preserve battery power by setting up a *power scheme* that turns off the monitor, the hard drive, or the entire computer after you have not used the computer for a while.

In Windows XP, right-click the 🔋 icon and then click **Adjust Power Properties**. In the Power Options Properties dialog box, click the **Power Schemes** tab and then either select a predefined power scheme from the Power Schemes list, or select specific times when XP should turn off the monitor or hard disks, or go into standby or hibernate mode.

In OS X, click 🔋 and then click **Open Energy Saver**. In the Energy Saver dialog box, click 🔽 to select a power scheme, or click and drag the sliders to set the amount of idle time after which OS X puts your computer or your display to sleep.

Configure Power Buttons

With Windows XP, you can configure your notebook power buttons to perform actions, such as sending your computer into standby or hibernate mode. This allows you to quickly initiate these actions.

There are three power buttons on most notebooks: the on/off (power) button, the sleep button, and closing the notebook lid. If your notebook does not have a sleep button, you can usually simulate one by tapping the on/off button quickly.

Right-click the 🔋 icon and then click **Adjust Power Properties**. In the Power Options Properties dialog box, click the **Advanced** tab. Use the lists in the Power buttons group to select the action that you want Windows to perform when you close the notebook lid, press the notebook on/off (power) button, or press the notebook sleep button.

Discover the Portable Computer Screen

Notebook computers use liquid crystal display (LCD) screens, which are the same type of display used in many cell phones, calculators, watches, and other electronic devices. An LCD produces images on the screen by shining light through liquid crystals and colored filters.

LCD Advantages

Compared to the cathode-ray tube (CRT) screens on most desktop monitors, LCD screens offer a number of advantages. They are thinner, which reduces the overall size of the portable computer. They weigh less, which increases the portability of the computer. They use far less power, which improves battery life. Moreover, they produce sharper text, which makes them easier to read.

Screen Size

The small overall size of a portable computer limits the size of the screen. The less expensive machines have display sizes between 10 and 12 inches (measured diagonally). Although the average size is 13 or 14 inches, many notebooks now have 15-inch screens, and even 17-inch screens are now available.

Passive Matrix

Many older notebooks use a *passive-matrix* type of LCD, which produces clear text, but is too slow to show videos and animations properly. Another drawback of passive-matrix displays is that they are often difficult to read at an angle, making them unsuitable for presentations to a group of people.

Today, although few notebook computers use passive-matrix displays, this type of display is still common in pagers, cell phones, and handheld computers that use a monochrome display.

Active Matrix

Most notebooks have an *active-matrix* LCD, which is sharper, brighter, and faster than a passive-matrix display. You can view active-matrix screens comfortably from wide angles. However, active matrix is also more expensive than passive matrix.

Active matrix is also called *thin film transistor* (TFT), because each pixel is controlled by one or more transistors, which increases the sharpness and speed of the display.

Upgrade with PC Cards

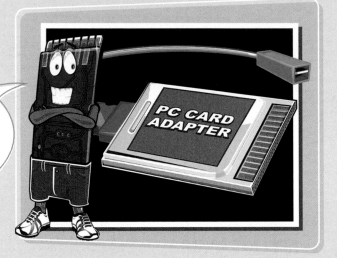

A PC Card is also called a Personal Computer Memory Card International Association card, or PCMCIA card.

A PC Card is a credit card-sized device that you insert into a special slot in your portable computer. You use PC Cards to upgrade your portable computer with devices such as network cards, wireless capabilities, and external storage.

PC Card Devices

You use PC Cards to add features to your portable computer. Possible devices that you can add using PC Cards include the following: memory, modem or fax/modem, wired or wireless network adapter, USB ports, FireWire ports, external disk drive, and sound card.

PC Card Types

PC Cards come in three general types. Type I cards can be up to 3.3 mm thick and are mostly used to add memory to a portable computer. Type II cards can be up to 5.5 mm thick and are most often used for input/output devices such as modems and network adapters. Type III cards can be up to 10.5 mm thick and are most often used for external disk drives.

PC Card Slot

Most portable PCs have one or two PC Card slots, and these slots vary by type. A Type I slot can hold one Type I card. A Type II slot can hold one Type II card or one Type I card. A Type III slot can hold one Type III card, two Type I cards, two Type II cards, or one each of a Type I and Type II card.

Insert a PC Card

To use a PC Card, insert the device into an empty PC Card slot on your notebook computer. Your computer speaker emits a beep and, if you have not inserted the PC Card before, the Found New Hardware Wizard appears. Insert the floppy disk or CD that came with the device and click **Next**. Windows XP installs the software for the device.

Remove a PC Card

When you no longer need a PC Card, you should remove it from your notebook computer. However, problems can arise if you do not allow Windows XP to shut down the device properly.

Click the Safely Remove Hardware icon (▣) in the taskbar's notification area. Windows XP displays a list of the devices that are attached to your notebook computer. Click the device that you want to remove. When Windows XP displays a message telling you that it is okay to remove the device, click the PC Card slot button to eject the device.

Chapter 9

Connecting to the Internet

Are you ready to take advantage of the rich diversity of the Internet, whether for education or entertainment? If so, then you need to understand what the Internet is about and how you can connect to it.

Introduction to the Internet

The Internet is a vast, worldwide network that enables you to read the latest news, to do research, to shop, to communicate, to listen to music, to play games, and to access a wide variety of information.

Origins

The Internet began in the late 1960s as a project sponsored by the U.S. Defense Department. Over time, the Internet expanded to include other government agencies, universities, research labs, and businesses.

Worldwide Network

The Internet is a worldwide network. Similar to a local area network, where you can work with shared resources on other computers, the Internet enables you to view and share information on other computers around the world.

Backbone

The Internet's backbone is a collection of telephone lines and fiber-optic cables that span the world. Data travels along this backbone at nearly the speed of light, so you can access data on the other side of the world in just seconds.

Internet Service Provider

An Internet service provider (ISP) is a company that has direct access to the Internet backbone. You can use a modem to access an ISP, which then connects you to the Internet.

Dial-Up Access

Dial-up Internet access uses a regular modem and a telephone line to connect to the Internet. Although dial-up accounts are inexpensive, they are also very slow.

Broadband Access

Broadband Internet access uses a high-speed modem to connect to the Internet. The connection is made through a digital subscriber line (DSL) telephone service or a television cable hookup. Broadband accounts are extremely fast, although they are more expensive than dial-up accounts.

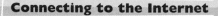

The World Wide Web

The World Wide Web is an interlinked collection of data. It is divided into separate *pages*, where each page has information on a specific topic. Most pages have at least one *link* that you can click to take you to a related page. There are billions of Web pages that cover millions of topics. For more information about the Web, see Chapter 10.

E-Mail

You can use electronic mail, or simply e-mail, to send and receive messages. Unlike postal mail messages, e-mail messages are delivered within minutes, and the cost is virtually free. For more information about e-mail, see Chapter 11.

Instant Messaging

You can use instant messaging to send and receive messages. These messages are exchanged instantly, similar to a conversation. For more information about sending and receiving instant messages, see Chapter 11.

Media

You can use the Internet to play songs and listen to radio stations. You can also run animations, view movie trailers, watch videos, and access many other types of media. For more information about multimedia, see Chapter 7.

Explore Internet Connections

Before you connect to the Internet, you need to know how to set up your modem, and how to choose an Internet service provider.

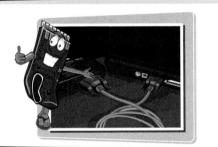

Serial Cable

You can attach this cable from the modem to the serial port in the back of your computer. You do not need to do this if your modem resides inside your computer case.

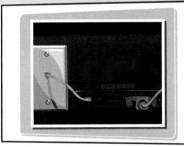

Phone Line

You can plug in a phone cord from the wall jack to the modem jack labeled *Line*. Some modem jacks are labeled *Telco*, or they show a picture of a wall jack instead of a label.

Telephone Connection

You can use a second phone cord to connect from the telephone to the modem jack labeled *Phone*. This jack usually shows a graphic of a telephone.

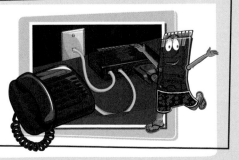

Internet Service Provider

You cannot access the Internet directly. Instead, to connect to the Internet, you must sign up for an account with an Internet service provider.

Connection Charges

An ISP charges you a monthly fee, which can range from a few dollars to $40 or $50 dollars per month. What you pay depends on the connection speed and how many minutes of connection time you are allowed each month. Keep in mind that most ISPs charge an extra fee per hour if you exceed your allotted time. To avoid extra fees, you may want to consider unlimited Internet access, which is offered by the majority of ISPs.

Connection Speed

Internet connections have different speeds, and these speeds determine how fast the Internet data is sent to your computer. If you connect to your ISP using a modem, the connection speed may be as low as 28.8 kilobits per second, although most ISPs now support modem speeds of up to 56 kilobits per second. You can obtain high-speed (or *broadband*) connections through either a television cable or an ADSL phone line. The ADSL connection offers speeds of over 1,000 kilobits per second, or 1 megabit per second.

Start the New Connection Wizard

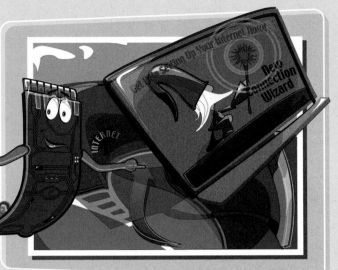

You can use the New Connection Wizard to help you connect to the Internet. The wizard guides you through a step-by-step process. This is much easier than trying to set up the connection on your own.

The New Connection Wizard offers you two ways to set up the connection: by choosing an ISP or by setting up the connection manually. This section shows you how to start the wizard, and the following sections take you through these two setup methods.

Start the New Connection Wizard

① Click **start**.

② Click **All Programs**.

③ Click **Accessories**.

④ Click **Communications**.

⑤ Click **New Connection Wizard**.

The New Connection Wizard appears.

⑥ Click **Next**.

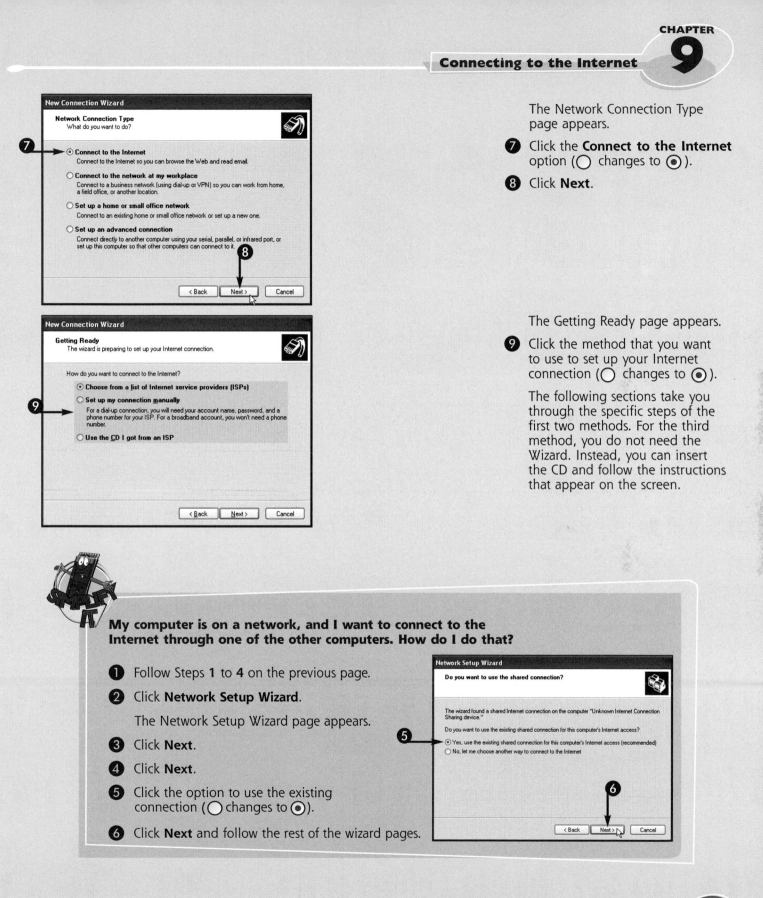

The Network Connection Type page appears.

7 Click the **Connect to the Internet** option (○ changes to ◉).

8 Click **Next**.

The Getting Ready page appears.

9 Click the method that you want to use to set up your Internet connection (○ changes to ◉).

The following sections take you through the specific steps of the first two methods. For the third method, you do not need the Wizard. Instead, you can insert the CD and follow the instructions that appear on the screen.

My computer is on a network, and I want to connect to the Internet through one of the other computers. How do I do that?

1 Follow Steps **1** to **4** on the previous page.

2 Click **Network Setup Wizard**.

The Network Setup Wizard page appears.

3 Click **Next**.

4 Click **Next**.

5 Click the option to use the existing connection (○ changes to ◉).

6 Click **Next** and follow the rest of the wizard pages.

Choose an Internet Service Provider

If you do not have an account with an Internet service provider, the New Connection Wizard can offer you a list of ISPs in your area.

Choose an Internet Service Provider

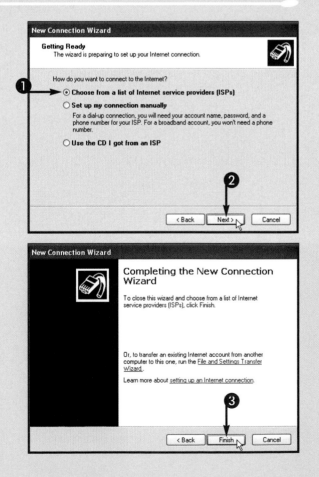

1 In the Getting Ready page of the New Connection Wizard, click the **Choose from a list of Internet service providers (ISPs)** option (○ changes to ◉).

2 Click **Next**.

The Completing the New Connection Wizard page appears.

In some versions of Windows XP, you must click the **Select from a list of other ISPs** option (○ changes to ◉).

3 Click **Finish**.

If the Online Services window appears, then double-click **Refer me to more Internet service providers**.

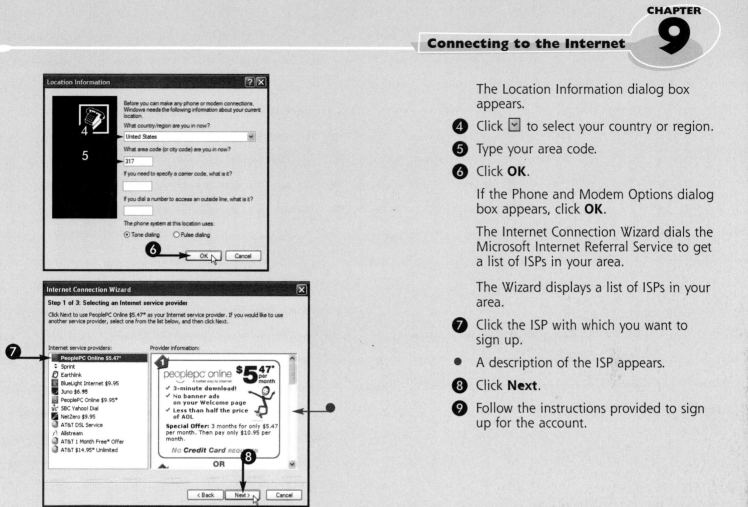

The Location Information dialog box appears.

④ Click ⊡ to select your country or region.

⑤ Type your area code.

⑥ Click **OK**.

If the Phone and Modem Options dialog box appears, click **OK**.

The Internet Connection Wizard dials the Microsoft Internet Referral Service to get a list of ISPs in your area.

The Wizard displays a list of ISPs in your area.

⑦ Click the ISP with which you want to sign up.

● A description of the ISP appears.

⑧ Click **Next**.

⑨ Follow the instructions provided to sign up for the account.

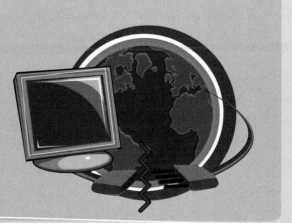

Can I cancel an ISP account if I decide to sign up with a different ISP?

Yes. Most ISPs allow you to manage your account online using the ISP home Web page. You can often cancel your account online, although most companies tend to make this option difficult to find. If you are having difficulty canceling your account online, you should be able to cancel the account by contacting the Customer Service department.

Set Up an Internet Connection

If you have already established an account with an ISP, you can manually set up your account by entering the information sent to you by your ISP.

Set Up an Internet Connection

SET UP A MODEM CONNECTION

① In the Getting Ready page of the New Connection Wizard, click **Set up my connection manually** (○ changes to ⦿).

② Click **Next**.

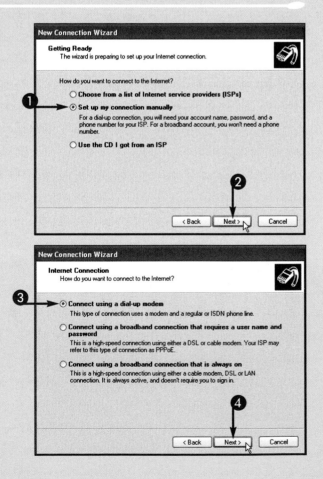

The Internet Connection page appears.

③ Click **Connect using a dial-up modem** (○ changes to ⦿).

If your account is a broadband connection with a username and password, click the **Connect using a broadband connection that requires a user name and password** option (○ changes to ⦿). You can then follow the remaining steps, except that you do not need to type a phone number.

④ Click **Next**.

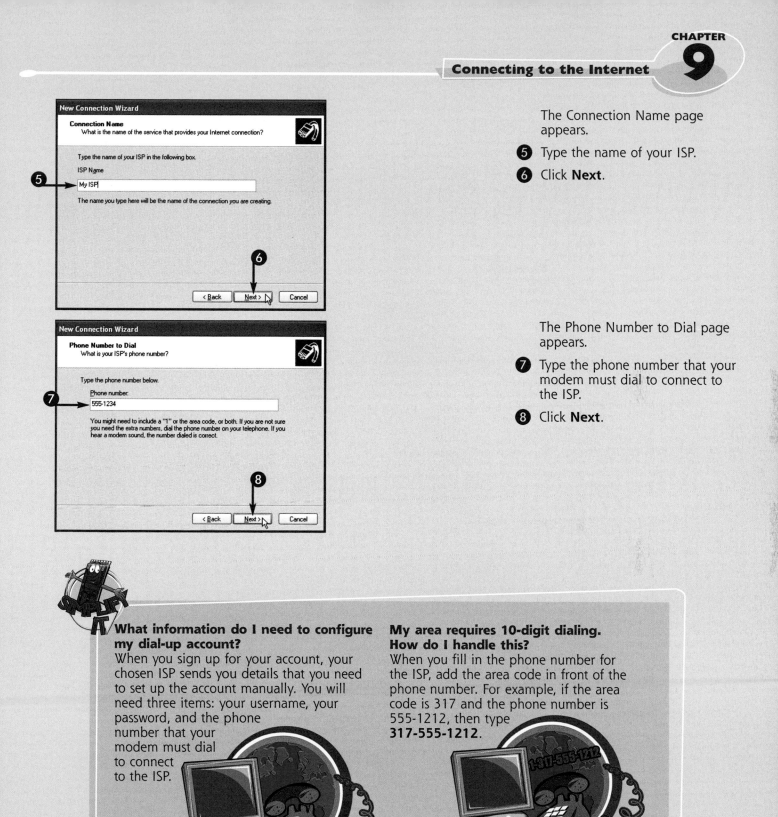

The Connection Name page appears.

5 Type the name of your ISP.

6 Click **Next**.

The Phone Number to Dial page appears.

7 Type the phone number that your modem must dial to connect to the ISP.

8 Click **Next**.

What information do I need to configure my dial-up account?
When you sign up for your account, your chosen ISP sends you details that you need to set up the account manually. You will need three items: your username, your password, and the phone number that your modem must dial to connect to the ISP.

My area requires 10-digit dialing. How do I handle this?
When you fill in the phone number for the ISP, add the area code in front of the phone number. For example, if the area code is 317 and the phone number is 555-1212, then type **317-555-1212**.

continued

Set Up an Internet Connection *(continued)*

With the Windows XP New Connection Wizard, it is easy for you to set up an account manually. It guides you step-by-step through the setup process.

Set Up an Internet Connection *(continued)*

The Internet Account Information page appears.

9 Type the username provided by your ISP.

10 Type your password.

● For security purposes, your password characters appear as dots.

If your password mixes uppercase and lowercase letters, then type the letters using the exact case specified by your ISP.

11 Type your password again.

12 Click **Next**.

The Completing the New Connection Wizard page appears.

● If you want to add the connection to your desktop as a shortcut icon, you can click **Add a shortcut to this connection to my desktop** (changes to).

13 Click **Finish**.

The Wizard configures your Internet account.

New Connection Wizard

Internet Account Information
You will need an account name and password to sign in to your Internet account.

Type an ISP account name and password, then write down this information and store it in a safe place. (If you have forgotten an existing account name or password, contact your ISP.)

User name: b1erej99 **9**

Password: ●●●●●●●● **10**

Confirm password: ●●●●●●●● **11**

☑ Use this account name and password when anyone connects to the Internet from this computer

☑ Make this the default Internet connection

12

[< Back] [Next >] [Cancel]

New Connection Wizard

Completing the New Connection Wizard

You have successfully completed the steps needed to create the following connection:

My ISP
* Make this the default connection
* Share with all users of this computer
* Use the same user name & password for everyone

The connection will be saved in the Network Connections folder.

☑ Add a shortcut to this connection to my desktop

13

To create the connection and close this wizard, click Finish.

[< Back] [Finish] [Cancel]

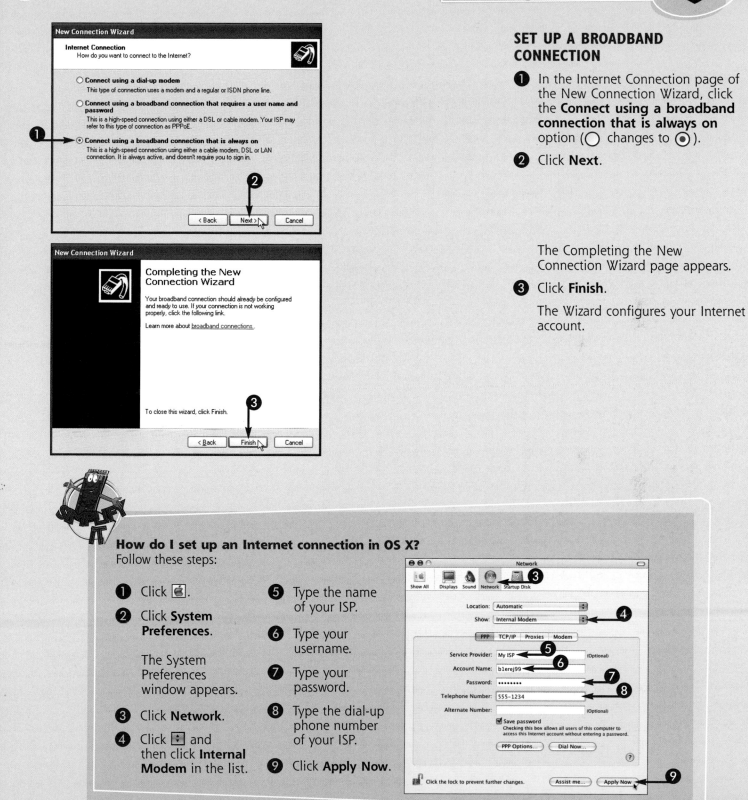

SET UP A BROADBAND CONNECTION

1 In the Internet Connection page of the New Connection Wizard, click the **Connect using a broadband connection that is always on** option (○ changes to ⊙).

2 Click **Next**.

The Completing the New Connection Wizard page appears.

3 Click **Finish**.

The Wizard configures your Internet account.

How do I set up an Internet connection in OS X?
Follow these steps:

1 Click .

2 Click **System Preferences**.

The System Preferences window appears.

3 Click **Network**.

4 Click and then click **Internal Modem** in the list.

5 Type the name of your ISP.

6 Type your username.

7 Type your password.

8 Type the dial-up phone number of your ISP.

9 Click **Apply Now**.

Connect to the Internet

Once you configure your Internet account, you can use it to connect to the Internet.

Connect to the Internet

① Click **start**.

② Click **Connect To**.

If you do not see the Connect To command, click **Control Panel**, then click **Network and Internet Connections**. Click **Network Connections**, and then double-click your Internet connection.

③ Click your Internet connection.

If you elected to place a connection shortcut on your desktop, you can also double-click that icon.

If your account requires a username and password, the Connect dialog box appears.

④ Click **Dial**.

Windows XP connects to the Internet.

● When the connection is complete, this icon appears in the taskbar notification area.

In OS X, click , click **System Preferences**, then click **Network**, and then click **Internal Modem**. Click **Connect**, and then click **Connect**.

Disconnect from the Internet

Many ISPs allow you a specified connection time per month, and they charge you a fee for each minute that you exceed your allotted time. Therefore, you should always disconnect when you are done to avoid additional connection charges.

After you have completed your Internet session, you should disconnect to avoid exceeding your allotted connection time.

Disconnect from the Internet

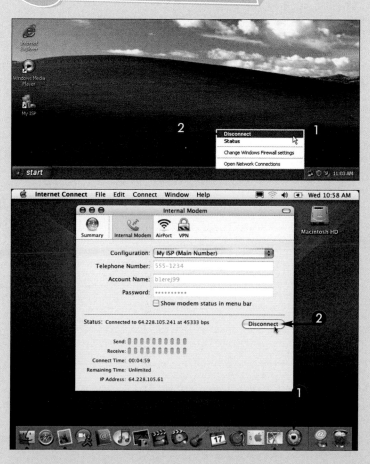

WINDOWS XP

① Right-click the connection icon (⬛).

② Click **Disconnect**.

Windows XP disconnects from the Internet.

OS X

① Click the **Internet Connect** icon (⬤).

The Internal Modem dialog box appears.

② Click **Disconnect**.

OS X disconnects from the Internet.

Make Your Internet Connection More Secure

When your computer is connected to the Internet, it is possible for another person on the Internet to access your computer and infect it with a virus or cause other damage. You can turn on the Windows XP Firewall, which prevents intruders from accessing your computer while you are connected to the Internet.

Windows XP Service Pack 2 has a Security Center, as shown in this section.

Make Your Internet Connection More Secure

❶ Click the Windows Security Alerts icon ().

If you do not see the Windows Security Alerts icon, click **start**, then click **All Programs**, and then click **Accessories**. Click **System Tools**, and then click **Security Center**.

The Windows Security Center window appears.

❷ Click the **Firewall** setting (🔘).

❸ If the Firewall setting is OFF, then click **Windows Firewall**.

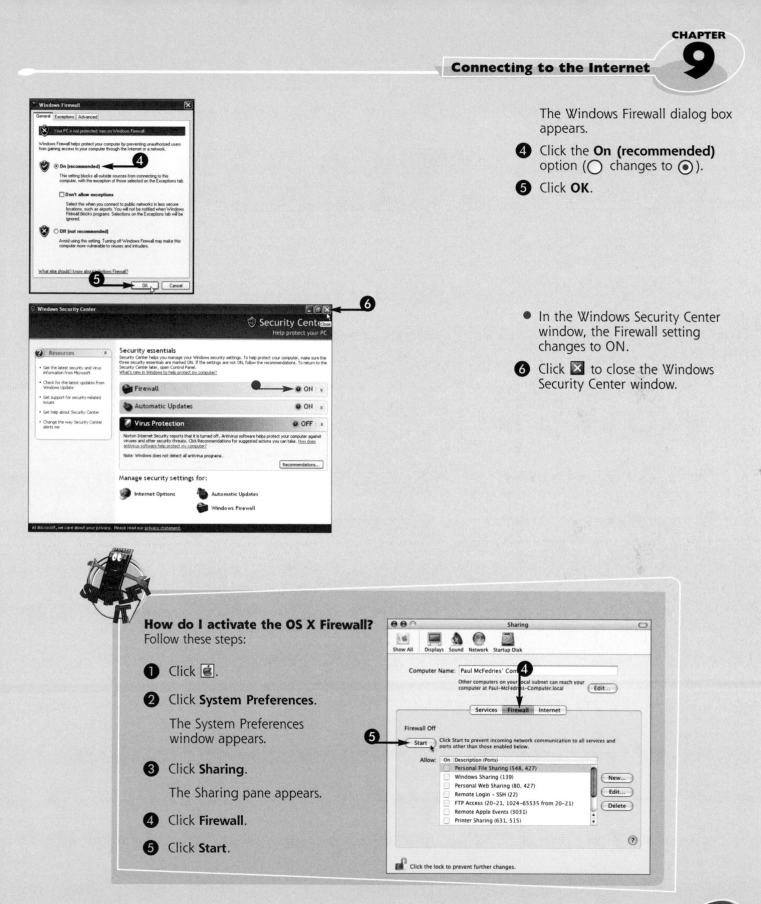

The Windows Firewall dialog box appears.

④ Click the **On (recommended)** option (○ changes to ◉).

⑤ Click **OK**.

● In the Windows Security Center window, the Firewall setting changes to ON.

⑥ Click ✕ to close the Windows Security Center window.

How do I activate the OS X Firewall?
Follow these steps:

① Click .

② Click **System Preferences**.

The System Preferences window appears.

③ Click **Sharing**.

The Sharing pane appears.

④ Click **Firewall**.

⑤ Click **Start**.

Chapter 10

Surfing the World Wide Web

After you set up your Internet connection, you can use the Windows XP Internet Explorer program to navigate, or *surf*, the Web sites on the World Wide Web. This chapter explains the Web and shows you how to navigate from site to site.

Introduction to the World Wide Web

The World Wide Web, or simply the Web, is a massive storehouse of information that resides on computers, called Web servers, located all over the world.

Web Page

World Wide Web information is presented on Web pages, which you download to your computer using a Web browser program, such as Windows XP Internet Explorer. Each Web page can combine text with images, sounds, music, and even videos to present you with information on a particular subject. The Web consists of billions of pages covering almost every imaginable topic.

Web Site

A Web site is a collection of Web pages associated with a particular person, business, government, school, or organization. Some Web sites deal with only a single topic, but most sites contain pages on a variety of topics.

Web Server

Web sites are stored on a Web server, which is a special computer that makes Web pages available for people to browse. A Web server is usually a powerful computer capable of handling thousands of site visitors at a time. The largest Web sites are run by *server farms*, which are networks that may contain dozens or even hundreds of servers.

Web Browser

A Web browser is a software program designed to download and display Web pages. Your operating system ships with a Web browser — Windows XP comes with Internet Explorer and Mac OS X comes with Safari — but there are other Web browsers that you can download.

Links

A link is a kind of cross-reference to another Web page. A link can appear as text that is usually underlined and in a different color from the regular text on the page. A link can also appear as an image. When you click the link, the page loads into your Web browser automatically. The link can take you to another page on the same site, or to a page on another Web site.

Web Address

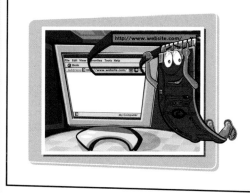

Every Web site and Web page has its own Web address that uniquely identifies the page. This address is the Uniform Resource Locator, or URL (pronounced *yoo-ar-ell* or *erl*). If you know the address of a page, you can type that address into your Web browser to view the page.

URL

The URL of a Web site or page is composed of four basic parts: the *transfer method* (usually http, which stands for HyperText Transfer Protocol), the *Web site domain name*, the *directory* where the Web page is located on the server, and the *Web page filename*.

The Web site domain name most often uses the .com (business) suffix, but other common suffixes include .gov (government), .org (nonprofit organization), and country domains such as .ca (Canada) and .uk (United Kingdom).

Learn About
Web Browsers

You can easily surf the Web if you know
your way around your Web browser.

Popular Web Browsers

Internet Explorer

Internet Explorer is the browser that comes with
Windows XP and most other versions of Windows,
as well as some versions of OS X. Internet Explorer
is by far the most popular Web browser. You can
find updates and more information at
www.microsoft.com/windows/ie/.

Safari

Safari is the browser that comes with the latest
versions of OS X — OS X 10.3, code-named
Panther, and OS X 10.4, code-named Tiger.
(Previous versions used a Macintosh version of
Internet Explorer.) You can find updates and more
information at www.apple.com/macosx/safari/.

Firefox

Firefox is a relatively new browser from the Mozilla
Foundation. Firefox is *open-source* software, which
means that it is a free program that was created
through a collaborative effort by a community of
programmers. Firefox is available for Windows and
OS X at www.mozilla.org/products/firefox/.

Web Browser Features

Web Page Title
The browser title bar displays the title of the displayed Web page.

Address Bar
This text box displays the address of the displayed Web page. You can also use the Address bar to type the address of a Web page that you want to visit.

Links
Links appear either as text or as images. On most pages, text links appear underlined and in a different color, usually blue, from the regular page text.

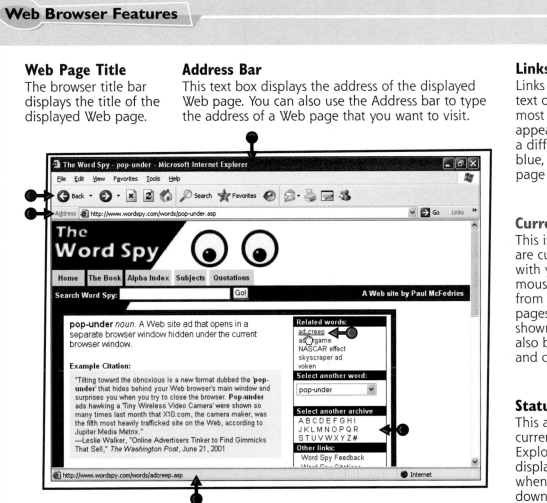

Current Link
This is the link that you are currently pointing at with your mouse. The mouse pointer changes from ↖ to ⊕. On some pages, such as the one shown here, the link text also becomes underlined and changes color.

Status Bar
This area displays the current status of Internet Explorer. For example, it displays Opening page when you are downloading a Web page, and Done when the page is fully loaded. When you point at a link, the Status bar displays the address of the page associated with the link.

Navigation Buttons
Each Web browser has navigation buttons that enable you to move back and forth through recently visited pages. For example, with Internet Explorer, you can click Back (⬅) to move to the previous page that you visited, and click Forward (➡) to move to the next page that you visited.

Search the Web

If you need information on a specific topic, there are free Web sites called search engines that enable you to quickly search the Web for pages that have the information that you require.

You can search the Web either by going directly to a search engine site or by using the search feature built into your browser.

Search Engine Sites

Here are the addresses of popular search engines:

Google	www.google.com
AltaVista	www.altavista.com
Ask Jeeves	www.ask.com
Excite	www.excite.com
HotBot	www.hotbot.com
Yahoo!	www.yahoo.com
MSN	www.msn.com

Web Browser Searching

To search the Web from Internet Explorer, click Search (🔍) to display the Search Companion; type a word, phrase, or question that you want to find; and then click **Search**. In Safari, click inside the Google Search box, type your search text, and then press `Return`. The Web browser then displays a list of links to sites that match your search text.

Web Crawler

Search engines index the Web by using special programs called *Web crawlers* — also called spiders or robots — to catalog each Web page and its content. Most search engines also enable individuals to submit information about their Web pages. Google, the largest search engine, indexes several billion Web pages.

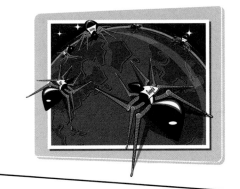

Search Strategies

The Web is so large that simple, one-word searches often return tens of thousands of *hits,* or matching sites. To improve your searching, enter multiple search terms that define what you are looking for. To search for a phrase, enclose the words in quotation marks. In addition, most search engines have advanced search capabilities that enable you to enter several terms and find sites that match at least one of the terms.

Search Types

By default, search engines return links to those Web pages that match your search criteria. However, the Web is about more than just text. It also contains images, music and audio files, video files, and news. Most of the larger search engines enable you to search for these different types of content.

Subject Directory

The Web is so large that many search engines have Web site directories that list sites by subject (such as Arts, Business, or Science). To ensure the quality of the information contained on each site, employees of the search engine usually review the sites listed in these subject directories.

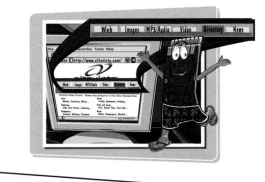

Read News on the Web

The Web is home to many sites that enable you to read the latest news. For example, many print sources have Web sites, some magazines exist only online, and there are more recent innovations such as Web logs.

Newspapers and Magazines

Print media such as newspapers and magazines have embraced the Web as a way to augment their traditional business. Some companies have Web sites with up-to-the-minute stories, whereas others use their sites just as archives of previously published stories. Some media sites require that you register in order to access the articles, but on most sites, the registration is free.

Online Magazines

A number of Web news sources exist only as online magazines, also called *e-zines*. The best of these online publications offer a wide variety of content and excellent writing. Some of the best are Salon (www.salon.com), Slate (www.slate.com), and Flak (www.flakmag.com).

Web Logs

A *Web log*, or *blog*, is a Web page consisting of frequently updated, reverse-chronological entries on a particular topic. Some blogs are mere diaries or lists of interesting links, but many have a news focus, particularly news on politics — such as Instapundit.com — and war — such as War and Piece (www.warandpiece.com).

News Portal

A *news portal* is a Web site that gathers news from hundreds or even thousands of online sources. You can then search the news, browse headlines, and view news by subject. Two popular news portals are NewsIsFree (www.newsisfree.com) and NewsNow (www.newsnow.co.uk). The major search engines also maintain news portals, such as Google News (news.google.com).

Syndication

Rather than surfing to a Web media site or news portal, you can have articles and news headlines sent to you. Many news sites use *syndication*, which enables a special program called an aggregator — also called an RSS reader (RSS is short for Real Simple Syndication) — to display the syndicated content. Firefox and the latest version of Safari have aggregators built in.

Research Using the Web

You can use the Web's vast resources to research just about any topic you can think of. The Web has information that can help you with a school project, your family history, or a presentation at work. You can search for the data that you need, or go to specific research sites.

Be aware that not all of the information on the Web is factual or useful. Sites often have inaccurate or deliberately misleading data. In general, stick to large, reputable sites.

Reference Materials

Sites such as Encarta (encarta.msn.com) and Britannica (www.britannica.com) offer multiple online research tools, including encyclopedias, dictionaries, and atlases. The Web is also home to thousands of sites that offer almanacs, maps, and thesauruses.

Libraries and Museums

Many public and private libraries maintain Web sites that enable you to search their catalogues, access their digital archives, and order books. There are also online libraries, such as the Internet Public Library (www.ipl.org), that catalog Internet sites. Many museums are also online, offering articles and interactive exhibits.

Government Resources

Federal, state, and municipal government Web sites contain a wealth of information on a wide variety of topics. Depending on the level of government, you can use these sites to research trends, statistics, regulations, laws and bylaws, patents, and trademarks. Most government sites also offer articles, papers, essays, and learning kits.

People and Genealogy

If you are trying to find a person, the Web has hundreds of sites that enable you to search for phone numbers, postal and e-mail addresses, and old classmates. If you are trying to find your ancestors, the Web also boasts hundreds of genealogy sites. Either you can search directly using online resources such as birth and death records, or you can use dedicated genealogy sites such as Ancestry.com and Genealogy.com.

Ask an Expert

Hundreds of millions of people access the Web, and many of them are experts on one or more topics. You can find many of these experts at "Ask an Expert" sites that enable you to pose questions that experts in the field will answer. Although some sites require a fee, many sites are free, including AllExperts (www.allexperts.com) and the Virtual Reference Desk (www.vrd.org/locator/).

Buy and Sell on the Web

There are many advantages to e-commerce. For buying, you have the convenience of shopping at home, easily comparing prices and features, and having goods delivered to your door. For selling, the Web offers low overhead and a potential audience of millions of people.

E-commerce — the online buying and selling of goods and services — is a big part of the Web. You can use Web-based stores to purchase books, theater tickets, and even cars. There are also many sites that enable you to sell or auction your products or household items.

Buying on the Web

Online Shopping

There are thousands of Web sites devoted to online shopping. Some, like Expedia Travel (www.expedia.com), focus on one product or service, whereas others, such as Amazon.com (www.amazon.com), offer a wide range of goods. You can also find Web sites for traditional retailers such as Wal-Mart and Pottery Barn, and many manufacturers enable you to purchase goods directly through their Web sites.

Shopping Cart

When you shop at an e-commerce site, you usually add the items that you want to purchase to a virtual *shopping cart* — also called a *shopping basket* — that keeps track of these items and the quantity. Most sites have a View Cart link that enables you to view the contents of your shopping cart. The cart usually has a Proceed to Checkout link that leads you to a page where you provide your address and payment information.

Product Reviews

If you are planning to make a purchase, whether it is a computer, a car, or a vacation, you can use the Web to research the product beforehand. There are sites devoted to product reviews by consumers, such as Epinions (www.epinions.com); reviews by companies, such as the J.D. Power Consumer Center (www.jdpower.com); and government resources, such as the Federal Citizen Information Center (www.pueblo.gsa.gov).

Site Security

Purchasing anything on the Web requires that you provide accurate payment data, such as your credit number and expiry date. To ensure that this sensitive data does not fall into the wrong hands, only provide this payment data on a secure site. Your browser may tell you when you are entering a secure site. Otherwise, look for "https" instead of "http" in the site address, and look for a lock icon in the browser window.

Selling on the Web

Virtual Store

Many Web companies offer *e-commerce hosting* to enable you to set up your own online store. Sites such as Yahoo! Small Business (smallbusiness.yahoo.com) and FreeMerchant (www.freemerchant.com) offer tools, storage space, and expertise to build and promote your store.

Online Auction

If you make your own products or have household items that you no longer need, you can put them up for sale in an online auction. By far, the most popular general online auction site is eBay (www.ebay.com), but there are also thousands of auction sites devoted to specific items, such as cars or memorabilia.

Many auction sellers accept payment through the PayPal service (www.paypal. com), which transfers buyer credit card payments to your bank account.

Socialize on the Web

The Web is generally a safe place to socialize, but, as in the real world, you should observe some common-sense precautions. For example, arrange to meet new friends in public places, supervise all online socializing done by children, and do not give out personal information to strangers.

The Web offers many opportunities to socialize, whether you are looking for a friend or a date or you just want some good conversation.

Meet Friends

If you are looking to meet new friends, either for the social contact or to expand your network, the Web has sites, such as MakeFriendsOnline (www.makefriendsonline.com), that enable you to meet people with common interests. Another popular site is Friendster.com, where you can meet new friends through your existing network of friends.

Find Dates

There are hundreds of online dating services that cater to all kinds of people looking for all kinds of relationships. Two of the most popular online dating sites are Lavalife (www.lavalife.com) and Match.com. There are also many sites devoted to specific types of people and relationships.

Discussion Boards

Many Web sites offer *discussion boards*, which are also called *message boards* or *forums*. These sections within the site enable visitors to post messages that are displayed on the site for others to see and to reply to. Some discussion boards deal with the site or company, such as the discussion boards on the eBay site, whereas others cover a particular subject, such as the numerous gardening forums hosted by GardenWeb.com.

Chat Rooms

A *chat room* is a section on a Web site in which visitors can exchange typed messages in real time. Depending on the popularity of the site, a chat room can contain anywhere from a few people chatting to a few dozen. Many chat services also enable you to switch to a "private" chat room for one-on-one discussions.

Pen Pals

In the real world, a pen pal is a person with whom you exchange letters. In the online world, a pen pal is someone with whom you exchange e-mail messages. Because e-mails are typed, online pen pals are sometimes called *keypals*. You can use the Web to find online pen pals, particularly for children. For example, see the KeyPals Club (www.teaching.com/keypals/) and ePALS (www.epals.com).

Chapter 11

Communicating Online

The Internet offers you a number of ways to communicate with other people, including e-mail messages, instant messages, and newsgroups.

Introduction to E-Mail

E-mail is the Internet system that enables you to electronically exchange messages with other Internet users anywhere in the world.

E-Mail Advantages

The e-mail system is nearly universal because anyone who can access the Internet has an e-mail address. E-mail is fast because messages are generally delivered within a few minutes — sometimes even just a few seconds — after being sent. E-mail is convenient because you can send messages at any time of day, and your recipient does not need to be at the computer or even connected to the Internet.

E-mail is inexpensive because you do not have to pay to send messages, no matter where in the world you send them. E-mail can also save you money because you can send a message instead of placing a long-distance phone call.

E-Mail Account

To use e-mail, you must have an e-mail account, which is usually supplied by your ISP. The account gives you an e-mail address to which others can send messages. See the section "Discover E-Mail Addresses" for more information.

You can also set up Web-based e-mail accounts with services such as Hotmail.com and Yahoo.com. A Web-based account is convenient because it enables you to send and receive messages from any computer.

How E-Mail Works

When you send an e-mail message, it travels along your Internet connection and then through your ISP's *outgoing mail server*. This server routes the messages to the recipient's *incoming mail server*, which then stores the message in that mailbox. The next time the recipient checks for messages, your message is moved from the recipient's server to the recipient's computer.

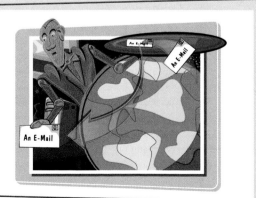

E-Mail Program

You can use an e-mail program to send and receive e-mail messages. Popular programs include Outlook Express (in Windows XP), Mail (in OS X), and Outlook (in Microsoft Office).

Messages
This area shows a list of the messages that are contained in the current folder.

Message Preview
This area shows a preview of the currently selected message.

Contacts
This area lists the people that you have added to your Address Book.

Folders
This area lists the program's folders, where it stores various types of messages:
● Inbox stores your incoming messages.
● Outbox stores outgoing messages that you have not sent.
● Sent Items stores outgoing messages that you have sent.
● Deleted Items stores messages that you have deleted from another folder.
● Drafts stores messages that you have saved but have not finished composing.

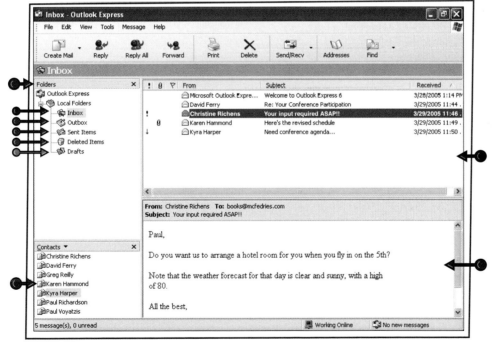

Discover E-Mail Addresses

You can only send an e-mail message to another person if you know that person's e-mail address.

An e-mail address is a set of characters that uniquely identifies the location of your Internet mailbox. A message sent to your address is delivered to you and no one else.

Parts of an E-Mail Address

Username
The username is the name of the person's account with the ISP or within their organization. This is often the person's first name, last name, or a combination of the two, but it could also be a nickname or some other text. No two people using the same ISP or within the same organization, can have the same username.

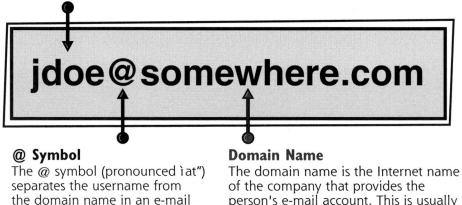

@ Symbol
The @ symbol (pronounced ìat") separates the username from the domain name in an e-mail address.

Domain Name
The domain name is the Internet name of the company that provides the person's e-mail account. This is usually the domain name of the ISP, an organization, or a Web e-mail service.

Multiple E-Mail Addresses

Most ISPs provide their customers with multiple mailboxes, each of which has its own e-mail address. This is useful if you want to provide separate addresses for each member of your family or business. You can also use multiple addresses, one for personal e-mail and another for mailing lists.

Address Book

You can use your e-mail program's address book to store the names and addresses of people with whom you frequently correspond. When you compose a message, you can then choose the recipient's name from the address book, and the program automatically adds the contact's e-mail address. This is both faster and more accurate than typing the address manually.

Invalid Address

If you make an error in the recipient's address and then send it, your message cannot be delivered. If you type a nonexistent domain name, your e-mail program will likely display an error message, such as "Unable to resolve domain name," when you try to send the message. If you type the wrong username, the message will go out, but you may receive a *bounce message* in return. Bounce messages report delivery errors. For an invalid username, you may receive a "No such user" or "Invalid recipient" error message.

Search for an E-Mail Address

You can use one of the Internet's *directory services* to find a person's e-mail address. A directory service, such as Yahoo! People Search (people.yahoo.com), is a kind of Internet white pages that enables you to look up an e-mail address when you know the person's first and last name.

Compose an E-Mail Message

If you know the e-mail address of a person or organization, you can send an e-mail message to that address. In most cases, the message is delivered within a few minutes.

If you do not know any e-mail addresses, or if at first you prefer to just practice sending messages, you can send messages to your own e-mail address.

E-Mail Style

Be Concise

Most of the time, e-mail contains short, to-the-point messages. This is particularly true in business, where most people use e-mail extensively. Therefore, being concise saves you time when composing a message, and it saves your recipient time when reading the message.

Check for Errors

Always thoroughly check your message for errors before you send it. Spelling mistakes, in particular, can mar an otherwise well-crafted message and obscure your meaning. Also, check your text for grammar mistakes and ambiguous words or phrases that could be misinterpreted. Finally, check that all your facts are accurate. Your goal should always be to write messages that are clean, clear, and correct.

Attachment

If you have a memo, image, or other document that you want to send to another person, you can attach the document to an e-mail message. The other person can then open the document after they receive your message.

Courtesy Copy

A *courtesy copy* is a copy of a message that you send to one or more people as a courtesy so that these people are aware of the contents of your message. In your e-mail program, you specify the main recipients in the "To" line and the courtesy copy recipients in the "Cc" line.

Smileys

The subtleties of humor and sarcasm are difficult to convey in print. To help prevent misunderstandings, people often use symbols, called *smileys* or *emoticons,* to convey an emotion or gesture. The word smiley comes from the following combination of symbols: :-), which looks like a smiling face if you tilt your head to the left.

Abbreviations

To save time writing and reading e-mail, many people use abbreviations — shortened forms of common phrases.

Receive an E-Mail Message

Your ISP's incoming mail server stores a message that is sent to you by another person. You must connect to the ISP's incoming mail server to retrieve new messages into your e-mail program.

Check for New Messages

All e-mail programs have a command that you can run to check for new messages on your ISP's incoming mail server. Make sure that you are connected to the Internet before you run this command. In addition, most e-mail programs automatically check the incoming mail server for new messages. For example, Outlook Express automatically checks for new messages every 30 minutes.

Spam and Viruses

Not all of the messages that you receive will come from people you know. Many unscrupulous businesses send *spam*, or unsolicited commercial e-mail. In addition, malicious users sometimes send computer viruses as e-mail attachments. For more information about spam and e-mail viruses, see Chapter 14.

Work with Received Messages

Store Messages

To keep your e-mail program's Inbox folder uncluttered, you can create new folders and then move messages from the Inbox to the new folders. You should use each folder that you create to save related messages. For example, you could create separate folders for each person with whom you correspond regularly, for projects that you are working on, and for different work departments.

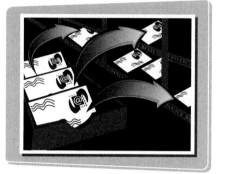

Reply to a Message

When a message that you receive requires some kind of response — whether it is answering a question, supplying information, or providing comments or criticism — you can reply to this message. To ensure that your correspondent knows which message you are responding to, include the relevant text from the original message in your reply.

Forward a Message

If a message has information that is relevant to or concerns another person, you can forward a copy of that message to that person. You can also include your own comments in the forward.

Learn About E-Mail Etiquette

To help make e-mail a pleasant experience for you and your correspondents, there are a few rules of e-mail etiquette — sometimes called netiquette, a blend of network and etiquette — that you should know.

Do Not SHOUT

Use the normal rules of capitalization in your e-mail text. In particular, AVOID LENGTHY PASSAGES OR ENTIRE MESSAGES WRITTEN IN CAPITAL LETTERS, WHICH ARE DIFFICULT TO READ AND MAKE IT APPEAR THAT YOU ARE SHOUTING.

Write Good Subjects

Busy e-mail readers often use a message's subject line to decide whether to read the message. This is particularly true if the recipient does not know you. Therefore, do not use subject lines that are either vague or overly general, such as "Info required" or "An e-mail message." Make your subject line descriptive enough so that the reader can tell at a glance what your message is about.

Quote Appropriately

When replying to a message, you can make sure that the other person knows what you are responding to by including quotes from the original message in your reply. However, quoting the entire message is usually wasteful, especially if the message is lengthy. Just include enough of the original message to put your response into context.

Keep Attachments Small

Avoid sending very large file attachments. If your recipient has a slow Internet connection, receiving the message can take an extremely long time. In addition, many ISPs place a limit on the size of a message's attachments, which is usually around 2 MB. In general, use e-mail to send only small files.

Get Permission

If you receive private e-mail correspondence from someone, it is considered impolite to quote the text of that message in another message or some other context. If you want to use that person's words, you must write to them and ask for permission.

Reply Promptly

When you receive a message in which the sender expects a reply from you, it is considered impolite to wait too long before responding. Whenever possible, urgent or time-sensitive messages should be answered within a few minutes to an hour. For other correspondence, you should reply within 24 hours.

Be Patient

E-mail is fast, but it is not meant for instantaneous communications. See the section "Communicate by Instant Messaging" for more information. If you send someone a message, do not expect an immediate response. Instead, expect the other person to take at least 24 hours to get back to you. If you have not heard back within 48 hours, it is okay to write a short note asking the person whether they received your message.

Do Not Send Flames

If you receive a message with what appears to be a thoughtless or insulting remark, your immediate reaction might be to compose an emotionally charged, scathing reply. Such a message is called a *flame*, and it will probably only make matters worse. Allow yourself at least 24 hours to cool down before responding to the message.

Communicate by Instant Messaging

Communicating in real-time means that if you send a message to another person who is online, that message appears on the person's computer right away. If that person sends you a response, it appears on your computer right away.

Instant messaging allows you to contact other people who are online, thus enabling you to have a real-time exchange of messages.

Instant Messaging Programs

To send and receive instant messages, you must use an instant messaging program. Windows XP comes with the Windows Messenger program; Mac OS X comes with iChat. Other programs include AOL Instant Messenger (www.aim.com), Yahoo! Messenger (messenger.yahoo.com), and ICQ (www.icq.com).

System Compatibility

The biggest problem with instant messaging systems is that they are generally not compatible with each other. With very few exceptions — for example, iChat works with AOL Instant Messenger — you cannot send instant messages between different systems. One solution is to download an all-in-one program such as Easy Message (www.easymessage.net) or Trillian (www.ceruleanstudios.com) that works with all instant messaging systems.

Contact List

You send instant messages to, and receive instant messages from, the people in your *contact list*, which is also called a *buddy list*. Your instant messaging program enables you to maintain your contact list by adding and deleting people, and it tells you the current online status of each person on the list.

Online Notification

Instant messages are "instant" because both parties are online at the same time, and so the program delivers the messages in real time. Therefore, most instant messaging programs notify you when a person who is in your contacts list comes online.

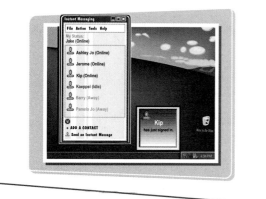

Online Status

If you do not want to receive any messages for a while, you can change your status accordingly. For example, Windows Messenger gives you six status settings, besides Online: Busy, Be Right Back, Away, On The Phone, Out To Lunch, and Appear Offline.

Block a Sender

If you no longer want to receive messages from a particular sender, all instant message programs enable you to block that sender. This means that the program will no longer allow messages from that person to go through. Blocking a sender is useful when that person becomes annoying, abusive, or offensive.

Carry On a Conversation

Before you can send or receive messages, you usually must add the other person as a contact in your instant messaging program, and that person must be online.

In instant messaging, a conversation is the exchange of text messages. Most instant messaging programs also enable you to exchange files or photos with the other person, as well as to have voice or video conversations.

Invite a Contact

Most instant messaging conversations begin by one person inviting another person to exchange messages. In most programs, this means sending an initial instant message, and the recipient either accepts the invitation by responding or rejects the invitation by ignoring the message.

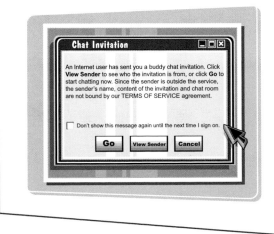

Respond to an Instant Message

When another person sends you an instant message, it shows up immediately in your instant messaging program. (If you are using AOL Instant Messenger, accept the Buddy Chat invitation by clicking **Go**.) To keep up your end of the conversation, you need to respond or send a new message of your own. Use the text box provided to type your message, and then click **Send** or press Enter or Return .

Send a File or Photo

Besides sending text messages, you can also use your instant messaging program to send documents, photos, or other files to a contact. This is useful if you want to discuss a file or photo with the other person or share your work with that person. For security reasons, the other person may choose not to accept the file that you send. You can also cancel your request to send a file before the other person accepts it.

Receive a File or Photo

If a person sends you a file through instant messaging, you can either accept or reject the file. If you accept the file, the instant messaging program automatically stores it on your computer's hard drive. Files can contain viruses, so be careful when someone requests to send a file to you. If you do not know the person, you should either reject the file transfer or scan the file with your antivirus software before opening it.

Place a Phone Call

If you and the contact with whom you want to converse both have a microphone attached to your computers, and a sound card and speakers, you can converse with each other just as though you were talking over the phone. Your instant messaging program probably has a *voice conversation* or *audio chat* feature that enables you to speak to another person over the Internet.

Carry on a Video Conversation

If you and the contact with whom you want to converse both have a Web camera, microphone, sound card, and speakers attached to your computer, you can both see and talk to each other at the same time. Some instant messaging programs have a *video conversation* or *video chat* feature that enables you to see each other's Web camera image and hear each other's voice.

Chapter 12

Wireless Computing

Many of the most common computing devices — particularly the keyboard and mouse — now come with wireless versions, enabling you to use these devices without connecting them directly to your computer. With other wireless equipment, you can also network computers and access the Internet without cables.

Discover Wireless Computing

Wireless computing allows you to operate your computer, communicate with others, and access resources — such as a network and the Internet — using equipment that does not require cables, phone lines, or any other direct, physical connection.

Wireless Advantages

The main advantage of wireless computing is the lack of cables, lines, and cords, which looks neater and makes devices easier to install. Wireless computing is also more flexible. For example, a wireless keyboard allows you to type a distance away from the computer; a notebook computer with a wireless network connection can usually allow you access to the network from anywhere in the same building.

Wireless Disadvantages

Wireless devices consume a great deal of power, which means that wireless peripherals require batteries, and wireless notebooks have shorter battery lives. In addition, interference from nearby devices can sometimes disrupt wireless communications, thus making them inconsistent. Finally, wireless networks are inherently less secure than wired networks, although there are precautions that you can take to enhance security.

Radio Signals

Wireless devices transmit data and communicate with other devices using radio signals that are beamed from one device to another. Although these radio signals are similar to those used in commercial radio broadcasts, they operate on a different frequency.

Radio Transceiver

A radio transceiver is a device that can act as both a transmitter and a receiver of radio signals. All wireless devices that require two-way communications use a transceiver. Devices that require only one-way communications — such as a wireless keyboard or mouse — have only a transmitter, and you attach a separate receiver to your computer.

Wireless Peripherals

You can operate your computer using wireless peripherals. To input data, you can use a wireless (often called *cordless*) keyboard, mouse, or joystick. To output data, you can use a wireless monitor or printer.

continued

Discover Wireless Computing *(continued)*

Wireless Networking

A wireless network is a collection of two or more computers that communicate with each other using radio signals. In an *ad hoc* wireless network, the computers connect directly to each other; in an *infrastructure* wireless network, the computers connect to each other through a common device, usually called an *access point*.

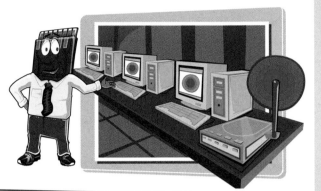

Wireless Internet

Many wireless access point devices have a port to which you can connect a high-speed modem. This enables the access point to establish its own Internet connection, and nearby wireless computers can then use the Internet through the access point.

Wireless Hotspots

A wireless *hotspot* is a location that allows wireless computers to use the location's Internet connection. You can find hotspots in many airports, hotels, and even businesses such as coffee shops, restaurants, and dental offices.

Wireless Technologies

The most common wireless technology is Wireless Fidelity, which is also called Wi-Fi (rhymes with hi-fi) or 802.11. There are four main types — 802.11, 802.11a, 802.11b, and 802.11g — each of which has its own range and speed limits. Another popular wireless technology is Bluetooth, which enables individual devices to automatically create *ad hoc* networks. Other examples of wireless technologies are cellular, microwave, and infrared.

Wireless Ranges

All wireless devices have a maximum range beyond which they can no longer communicate with other devices. Peripherals such as keyboards have a range of only a few feet. In practice, Wi-Fi networking ranges span from 75 feet for 802.11a to about 150 feet for 802.11b and 802.11g.

Wireless Speeds

Wireless transmission speed — which is usually measured in megabits per second, or Mbps — is an important factor to consider when you set up a wireless network or a wireless Internet connection. Less expensive wireless networks most often use 802.11b, which has a theoretical top speed of 11 Mbps. The increasingly popular 802.11g standard has a theoretical speed limit of 54 Mbps.

Wireless Computing Devices

Wireless computing requires devices that have wireless capabilities. Although wireless capabilities are built in to many of today's notebook computers, in most cases you will need to purchase additional wireless devices, depending on the kinds of wireless computing that you want to use.

Wireless Input

Outside of networking, the most common wireless products today are input devices, particularly the keyboard and mouse. You attach a USB transceiver to your computer, and the keyboard and mouse can operate within 20 or 30 feet of the transceiver.

Other Wireless Peripherals

Another common wireless device is a wireless print server to which you attach a regular printer; it allows all the wired and wireless computers on your network to access the printer. Other wireless peripherals include monitors, Web cams, printers, game pads, and transmitters that beam digital music from your PC to your stereo.

Wireless Handhelds

Handheld devices often have either Wi-Fi or Bluetooth wireless capabilities built in. This enables these devices to take advantage of hotspots, to check e-mail, or to surf the Web, as well as to synchronize with desktop computers.

Wireless Network Adapters

To access a wireless network, your computer requires a wireless network adapter.

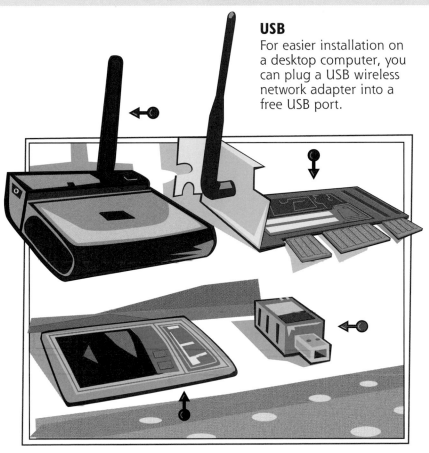

USB
For easier installation on a desktop computer, you can plug a USB wireless network adapter into a free USB port.

Network Interface Card
You can insert a wireless network interface card (NIC) into your desktop computer.

PC Card
For notebook computers that do not have built-in wireless capabilities, you can insert a PC Card.

Bluetooth Adapter
To set up an *ad hoc* network with any Bluetooth device, your computer requires a Bluetooth adapter, most of which plug into a USB port.

Wireless Access Point
A wireless access point (AP) is a device that receives and transmits signals from wireless computers to form a wireless network. Many APs also accept wired connections, which enables both wired and wireless computers to form a network. If your network has a broadband modem, you can connect the modem to a type of AP called a wireless gateway, which extends Internet access to all the computers on the network.

Wireless Range Extender
If you find that your wireless access point is not reaching certain areas of your home or office, you can use a wireless range extender to boost the signal. Depending on the device and wireless access point, the extender can more than double the normal wireless range.

Connect to a Wireless Network

With your wireless network adapters installed and your wireless gateway or access point configured, you are ready to connect to your wireless network. This will give you access to the network's resources, as well as to the Internet if you have a wireless gateway.

Connect for the First Time

After you initially set up a computer for wireless networking, or if you move your portable computer to a hotspot or other area with new networks in range, your computer will display a list of the available wireless networks. Connect to the network that you want to use.

Connect to a Secure Network

If the network that you want to use is unsecured — as are most public hotspots — then you can immediately access the network. However, most private wireless networks are secured against unauthorized access. In this case, the network will ask you to enter the appropriate security information.

View Available Networks

If you take your portable computer to a public place, such as a hotel, airport, or coffee shop, there may be a nearby wireless network that offers Internet access. You can use your computer to display a list of available wireless networks. In Windows XP, right-click the Wireless Network Connection icon () in the notification area, and then click **View Available Wireless Networks**.

Reconnect to a Wireless Network

If you lose your wireless network connection, you must reconnect to continue using it. One way to do this is to display the list of available wireless networks and then connect to the one that you want. However, in Windows XP, you can also click **start,** then click **Connect To,** and then click **Wireless Network Connection**.

View Signal Strength

If you are having problems with a wireless network connection, check the signal strength. In Windows XP, place the mouse ⌖ over the 📶 icon in the taskbar. Alternatively, double-click the icon to display the Wireless Internet Connection Status dialog box.

Disconnect from a Wireless Network

When you no longer need a wireless network connection, or if you want to try a different available network, you should disconnect from the current network. Display the list of available wireless networks, click the network to which you are connected, and then click **Disconnect**.

Chapter 13

Performing Computer Maintenance

To keep your system running smoothly, to maintain top performance, and to reduce the risk of computer problems, you need to perform some routine maintenance chores. You need to update the operating system, check for hard drive errors, defragment your hard disk, and back up your files.

Update Your Operating System

In Windows XP, you must be logged on with an Administrator account to update your system.

To update your operating system, you need to download and install the latest components and programs. These updates fix problems and resolve security issues. You can reduce computer problems and maximize online safety by updating your operating system regularly.

Update Types

Bug Fixes

Operating systems sometimes have glitches — usually called *bugs* — that cause the system to behave erratically or crash. Many operating system updates are designed to fix these problems and to make your system run smoother.

Security Updates

Some operating system problems can lead to security breaches that might enable another person to infiltrate your system or infect it with a virus. Most operating system updates are plugs for these security holes.

Updating Windows XP

Manual Updates

You can update Windows XP at any time. To do so, connect to the Internet and then click **start,** then click **All Programs,** and then click **Windows Update**. This takes you to the Windows Update Web site. Click the **Express Install** link to start the process.

Automatic Updates

Most Windows XP systems are set up to download and install updates automatically. To ensure that your system is set up to do this, click **start**, right-click **My Computer**, and then click **Properties**. In the System Properties dialog box, click the **Automatic Updates** tab, and then click **Automatic** (◯ changes to ◉).

Updating Mac OS X

Manual Updates

You can update Mac OS X manually. To do so, connect to the Internet, click , and then click **Software Updates**. OS X checks for new updates and displays the results in the Software Update window. Activate the check boxes (☐ changes to ☑) for the items that you want to install, and then click **Install**.

Automatic Updates

Most OS X systems are set up to check for updates automatically. To configure automatic update checking on your system, click **Software Update** and then click **Preferences**. Activate the **Check for updates** check box (☐ changes to ☑), click , and then click the frequency you prefer (such as Weekly). If you want critical updates to download automatically, then activate the Download important updates in the background check box (☐ changes to ☑).

Check Your Hard Drive for Errors

Hard drive errors can cause files to become corrupted, which may prevent you from running a program or opening a document. Your operating system has a program that you can use to look for and fix hard drive errors.

Hard Drive Error Types

Bad Sector

Your hard drive is divided into small storage areas called *sectors*, which usually hold up to 512 bytes of data. A bad sector is one that — through physical damage or some other cause — the operating system can no longer use to reliably store data.

File System Error

Because the operating system stores each file in multiple parts on the hard drive, one of the operating system's most important jobs is to keep track of each part of every file. A *file system error* occurs when the operating system loses track of part of a file or mixes up the parts of two or more files.

Windows XP

To check your hard drive for errors with Windows XP, click **start**, click **My Computer**, right-click the hard drive that you want to check, and then click **Properties**. In the hard drive's Properties dialog box, click the **Tools** tab, and then click **Check Now**. Use the Check Disk dialog box to run the check.

OS X

To check your startup hard drive for errors with OS X, insert your OS X Install Disc and reboot from that disc. (Click , click **System Preferences**, click **Startup Disk**, click the Install Disc icon, and then click **Restart**.) When the Installer appears, click **Installer**, and then click **Open Disk Utility**. In the Disk Utility window, click **Macintosh HD**, and then click **Verify Disk**.

Third-Party Programs

There are third-party programs available that can check for and repair hard drive errors. Popular programs include Norton SystemWorks (www.symantec.com) and VCOM's Fix-It Utilities (www.v-com.com).

Frequency

You should perform the hard drive check about once a week. Perform Windows XP's more thorough bad-sector check once a month. Keep in mind that the bad-sector check can take several hours, depending on the size of the drive, and so you should only perform this check when you do not need your computer for a while.

Defragment Your Hard Drive

To *defragment* your *hard drive* means to bring together the various pieces *that* comprise each *file* on the *drive*. This makes your *operating system* and your *programs* run faster, and also makes your *documents* open *more* quickly.

Understanding Defragmentation

Clusters

Hard drives typically contain billions of sectors, and so it would be too inefficient for the operating system to deal with individual sectors. Instead, the operating system groups sectors into *clusters*, the size of which depends on the size of the disk, although 4KB is typical.

Defragmentation

When the operating system saves a file to the hard drive, it generally looks for the first available cluster and stores part of the file there, another part in the next available cluster, and so on. Over time, the various cluster-sized pieces of a file often become scattered around your hard drive. Defragmenting improves performance by bringing all of those pieces together, which makes finding and opening each file faster.

Windows XP

To defragment your hard drive with Windows XP, click **start**, click **My Computer**, right-click the hard drive that you want to check, and then click **Properties**. In the hard drive's Properties dialog box, click the **Tools** tab, and then click **Defragment Now**. In the Disk Defragmenter window, click the hard drive and then click **Analyze** to see whether the drive is defragmented. If the program recommends defragmenting, click **Defragment**.

Third-Party Programs

There are third-party programs available that can defragment your hard drive. Popular programs include Diskeeper (www.executive.com) for Windows XP and Norton Utilities (www.symantec.com) for OS X (which does not have a built-in defragmenter).

Frequency

How often you defragment your hard drive depends on how often you use your computer. If you use your computer every day, then you should defragment your hard drive once a week. If you use your computer only occasionally, then you should defragment your hard drive every two or three months.

Clean Up Your Hard Drive

To clean your hard drive means to free up space by deleting files that your system no longer needs. This helps to ensure that your system runs efficiently.

If you run out of room on your hard drive, you cannot install more programs or create more documents.

Unnecessary Files

Downloaded Program Files	Small Web page programs that are downloaded onto your hard drive
Temporary Internet Files	Web page copies that are stored on your hard drive for faster viewing
Offline Web Pages	Web page copies that are stored on your hard drive for offline viewing
Microsoft Error Reporting Temporary Files	Files that are used by the Microsoft Error Reporting service
Office Setup Files	Installation files that are used by Microsoft Office
Recycle Bin	Files that you have deleted recently
Temporary Files	Files that are used by programs to store temporary data
WebClient/Publisher Temporary Files	Copies of files that are used to improve the performance of the WebClient/Publisher service
Temporary Offline Files	Local copies of recently used network files
Offline Files	Local copies of network files that are made available offline
Catalog Files for the Content Indexer	Old files that were once used to speed up file searches

Windows XP

To clean up your hard drive with Windows XP, click **start**, click **My Computer**, right-click the hard drive that you want to check, and then click **Properties**. In the hard drive's Properties dialog box, click **Disk Cleanup**. Click the check box (☐ changes to ☑) for each file type that you want to delete. Click **OK** and then click **Yes**.

Third-Party Programs

There are a number of third-party programs available that can delete unneeded files and programs from your hard drive. Popular programs include McAfee QuickClean (www.mcafee.com) for Windows XP and Spring Cleaning (www.allume.com) for both Windows XP and Mac OS X.

Frequency

Clean up your hard drive whenever the drive's free space becomes too low. If hard drive space is not a problem, clean up the hard drive every two or three months.

To check the amount of hard drive free space that you have in Windows XP, click **start**, click **My Computer**, and then click the hard drive. In the Task pane, the Details area shows the amount of free space.

Back Up Your Files

If you use Windows XP, be sure to at least back up your My Documents folder to keep your document safe. If you use OS X, back up the Documents folder.

To back up your files means to create copies of those files and to store those copies in a safe place. If a system problem causes you to lose one or more files, you can restore them from the backup.

Backup Media

Although you can back up files to floppy disks, they can only hold a small amount of data. You can save time by backing up to a storage medium that has a greater capacity. For example, you can back up to a Zip disk, a second internal hard drive, an external hard drive, a flash drive, a network folder, or a tape drive.

Backup Types

The backup type determines which files are included in the backup job. A *normal* backup includes every file; an *incremental* backup includes only those files that have changed since the most recent normal or incremental backup; a *differential* backup includes only those files that have changed since the most recent nondifferential backup; a *daily* backup includes only those files that are modified on the day that you run the backup; a *copy* backup makes copies of the files.

Windows XP

To back up files with Windows XP Professional, click **start**, click **My Computer**, right-click the hard drive that you want to back up, and then click **Properties**. In the hard drive's Properties dialog box, click the **Tools** tab, and then click **Backup Now**. Use the Backup or Restore Wizard to guide you through the backup steps.

Third-Party Programs

There are a number of third-party programs available that can back up your files. Popular programs include Norton Ghost (www.symantec.com) for Windows XP and Retrospect (www.dantz.com) for both Windows XP and OS X.

Frequency

To avoid losing data because of a system crash or other problem, you should back up your important files regularly. A good strategy is to run a daily backup each day, to run an incremental backup once a week, and to run a normal backup once a month. After you complete the normal backup, delete the previous month's daily, incremental, and normal backups.

Restore

You can restore a file from a backup if the file is lost because of a system problem or because you accidentally deleted or overwrote the file. All backup programs have a Restore feature that enables you to choose the files that you want to restore.

Chapter 14

Implementing Computer Security

Threats to your computer-related security and privacy often come from the Internet in the form of system intruders, such as e-mail spam, viruses, and identity thieves. In addition, many security and privacy violations occur right at your computer by someone simply logging in to your computer while you are not around. To protect yourself and your family, you need to understand these threats and to know what you can do to thwart them.

STOP

ACME
Firewall
SOFTWARE

ACME
**Content
Filter**

Filter Web sites
Limit Online Sessions
Record Chats
Block Newsgroups

Security
✓ Do not allow unknown
   attachments to be
   saved or opened
✓ Do not open file types
   that may carry viruses

Guard Against Internet Intruders

You can set up your computer or network to prevent such intrusions.

An Internet intruder is a person who attempts to gain access to your computer or network through your Internet connection. The intruder's goal is to examine your confidential data, to destroy files, to install a virus, or to steal your passwords.

Firewall

A *firewall* is a software program, device, or computer that restricts the type of data that can pass from the Internet to a person's computer or network. In this way, the firewall prevents unauthorized users from gaining access to the computer or network.

Firewall Types

A software firewall is a program that protects a computer from Internet intruders by blocking the virtual ports that outsiders can use to view and access the computer. A hardware firewall is a device that protects a computer or a network from intrusion. Many routers and wireless gateways have firewall features built in. On larger networks, a powerful computer usually implements the firewall.

Windows XP Firewall

Windows XP has a built-in firewall program. To ensure that it is turned on, click **start,** click **All Programs,** and then click **Accessories.** Click **System Tools,** and then click **Security Center**. In the Windows Security Center window, make sure that the Firewall setting is On. If the setting is Off, click **Windows Firewall** and then click **On** (○ changes to ◉).

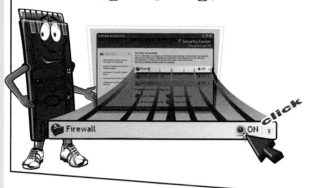

OS X Firewall

OS X has a built-in firewall program. To ensure that it is turned on, click , click **System Preferences**, and then click **Sharing**. In the Sharing window, click **Firewall**. If the firewall is off, click **Start**.

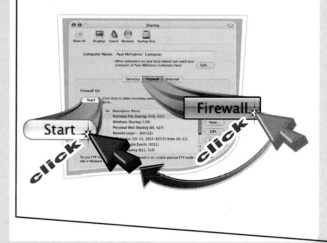

Third-Party Firewalls

You can install a number of third-party firewall programs, most of which offer more features than the program that ships with your operating system. The most popular firewalls are ZoneAlarm (www.zonelabs.com) for Windows XP and Norton Personal Firewall (www.symantec.com) for Windows XP and OS X.

Test Your Firewall

To ensure that your firewall is working correctly, there are Internet sites that can test it for you. Try Gibson Research Corporation's Shields UP (www.grc.com) or HackerWhacker (www.hackerwhacker.com).

Protect Yourself on the Web

Protecting yourself on the Web means understanding and preventing a number of security and privacy problems. These include problems with spyware, pop-up ads, saved passwords, cookies, and insecure sites.

Spyware

Spyware is a software program that installs on your computer without your knowledge or consent. This program surreptitiously gathers data from your computer, steals your passwords, displays advertisements, and hijacks your Web browser. To eliminate the program from your computer and prevent spyware from installing on your computer, use a program such as Ad-Aware (www.lavasoft.com) or Windows AntiSpyware (www.microsoft.com/athome/security/spyware/).

Pop-Up Ads

A *pop-up ad* is an advertisement that interrupts your Web browsing by appearing in a separate browser window on top of your current window. Pop-ups are annoying, but also dangerous because clicking items in the pop-up window can cause spyware to be installed on your computer. Use a pop-up blocker such as the ones built into Internet Explorer and Firefox.

Saved Passwords

When you submit a form that includes a site password, Internet Explorer displays a prompt that offers to remember the password. If you click **Yes** and then access the site at a later date, Internet Explorer bypasses the login page and takes you directly to the site. Unfortunately, this also means that anyone else who uses your computer can access the site. Therefore, you may want to click **No** when Internet Explorer asks to remember the password.

Cookies

A *cookie* is a small text file that a Web site stores on your computer to keep track of things such as preferences and shopping cart items. Cookies can also store site usernames and passwords, as well as your credit card data; if possible, tell the site not to save this data. Alternatively, use a cookie manager program such as Cookie Crusher (www.thelimitsoft.com) or Cookie Pal (www.kburra.com).

Insecure Sites

Secure Site Indicators

Information that you send over the Web — such as when you fill out and send a form — is usually sent in plain text that anyone can read. A secure site is one that sends your data in an encrypted format that is impossible to read. Before you send sensitive data such as your credit card number, be sure that the site is secure. Look for "https" in the address bar and a lock icon in the status bar.

Secure Site Warnings

To help you know when you are entering a secure site, browsers such as Internet Explorer and Firefox display a warning dialog box. More importantly, these browsers also display a warning dialog box when you leave a secure site.

Protect Your Children on the Web

It is very easy for children to come upon inappropriate material on the Web, even inadvertently. You should not underestimate the level of protection that they need.

To protect your children on the Web means to understand the dangers that await your children and to learn ways to avoid those dangers.

Potential Dangers

Images

The Web has no shortage of explicit or violent images that are not suitable for children. Sites that display such images usually require membership or payment, but some do not, and those sites often display unsuitable images on their home pages.

Information

The Web is a massive storehouse of knowledge, not all of which is benign. There are sites where the content uses profanity, and other sites that offer inappropriate information on topics ranging from mixing chemicals to making weapons.

Chat Rooms

Adults who desire to meet young children often frequent Internet chat rooms and attempt to get young participants to reveal personal details about themselves, particularly where they live or where they go to school.

Ways to Protect Children

Restrict Content

Many Web browsers have features that restrict certain types of inappropriate Web content to authorized users. These restrictions are based on ratings that are applied to certain sites.

In Internet Explorer, select **Tools,** click **Internet Options**, click the **Content** tab, and then click **Enable**. Use the Content Advisor to set the maximum levels for language, nudity, sex, and violence that unauthorized users can access.

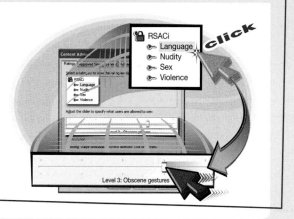

Third-Party Programs

Many third-party programs filter out content deemed objectionable to children. Among the most popular in this category are Cybersitter (www.cybersitter.com), Net Nanny (www.netnanny.com), and CyberPatrol (www.cyberpatrol.com).

Supervision and Education

Ideally, parents should also be directly involved in protecting their children on the Web. For very young children, parents should supervise Web sessions to prevent access to inappropriate content. For older children, parents should educate them on the potential dangers and lay down ground rules for using the Web (such as not giving out personal data to strangers without permission).

Reduce E-Mail Spam

A *spam* is an unsolicited, commercial e-mail message that advertises anything from a baldness cure to cheap printer cartridges. Most people receive at least a few *spams* a day; some people receive hundreds of them. No matter how many you receive, reducing *spam* can save time and reduce e-mail frustration.

Some *spams* are more than just annoying. For example, many *spams* advertise deals that are simply fraudulent, and others feature such unsavory practices as linking to adult-oriented sites and sites that install *spyware*.

Do Not Open Spam

Never open suspected spam messages, because doing so can sometimes notify the spammer that you have opened the message.

Notifying the spammer in this way is a big problem because it confirms that the message was delivered to you successfully. This proves to the spammer that your address is legitimate, and so you will likely receive even more spam.

Do Not Respond to Spam

Never respond to spam, even to an address within the spam that claims to be a "removal" address. If you respond to the spam, all you are doing is proving that your address is legitimate.

Similarly, never click a Web site link that appears within a spam. At best, clicking the link may prove that your address is active. At worst, the link may take you to a site that displays objectionable content or that surreptitiously installs spyware on your computer.

Disable E-Mail Images

A *Web bug* is an image embedded in a spam that downloads from the spammer's Web site, even if you simply preview the message. This tells the spammer that your address is active. Many e-mail programs enable you to disable e-mail images.

For example, in Outlook Express, click **Tools**, click **Options**, click the **Security** tab, and then click **Block images and other external content in HTML e-mail** (☐ changes to ☑).

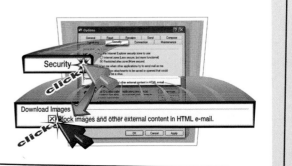

Alter Your Newsgroup Address

The most common method that spammers use to gather addresses is to harvest them from newsgroup posts. Therefore, never use your actual e-mail address in a newsgroup account.

If you want other newsgroup users to be able to e-mail you, one common solution is to alter your newsgroup e-mail address by adding text that invalidates the address but is still obvious for other people to figure out.

Use a Fake Web Address

When you sign up for something online, use a fake address if possible. If you must use your real address because you need or want to receive e-mail from the company, then make sure that you deselect any options that ask whether you want to receive promotional offers.

Another solution is to supply the site with the address from a free Web-based account (such as a Hotmail account) so that any spam that you receive is sent there instead of to your main address.

Anti-Spam Software

A number of companies offer anti-spam programs that do a good job of filtering out most junk e-mail. Some popular programs in this category are Norton AntiSpam (www.symantec.com) and McAfee SpamKiller (www.mcafee.com).

Guard Against E-Mail Viruses

A *virus is* a malicious program that can crash your computer or damage your files. Most *viruses* propagate through e-mail in the form of attachments. When you open the attachment, the *virus* infects your computer. You can take a few simple precautions to avoid *virus* infections.

Large-scale virus outbreaks occur because some viruses surreptitiously use your e-mail program and your address book to send out messages with more copies of the virus attached.

Attachments from Strangers

There is no reason why a stranger should send you an attachment. If you receive a message that has an attachment, and you do not know the sender of the message, then do not open the attachment.

Attachments from Friends

If a friend unexpectedly sends you a message with an attachment, do not assume that the attachment is benign. The friend's computer may be infected with a virus that e-mails copies of itself. Send a message to your friend to confirm that they actually sent the file.

Read in Plain Text

The HTML message format uses the same codes that create Web pages. Therefore, just as some Web pages are unsafe, so are some e-mail messages. This is because they can contain malicious scripts that run automatically when you open or even just preview a message.

You can prevent these scripts from running by changing your e-mail program settings to read all your messages in the plain text format. You can do this in most e-mail programs, including Outlook Express, Microsoft Outlook, and OS X Mail.

E-Mail Program Security

Most e-mail programs offer security against viruses. For example, the program may come with a setting that prevents other programs from sending mail using your account. Activating this setting thwarts those viruses that try to replicate themselves using your e-mail program.

Another common security setting is to prevent the opening of file types that commonly carry viruses. These file types include script files, executable files, batch files, and even screen savers, which can carry malicious code.

Antivirus Software

It is important to install a good antivirus program on your system, particularly a program that checks all incoming messages for viruses. Try Norton AntiVirus (www.symantec.com) or McAfee VirusScan (www.mcafee.com).

Index

Index

digital cameras
  defined, 20
  features, 111, 113
  megapixels, 110, 112
  memory, 111
  photo transfer, 111
  storage, 113
  uses, 110, 112
  video transfer, 113
digital pen/stylus, 59
digital sampling, 122
digital versatile disc drives. *See* DVD drives
digital video, 120–121
discussion boards, 169
disk drives, 16
displays. *See* monitors
document scanners, 20
documents
  bullets, 96
  changes, 78
  creating, 6
  grammar, 97
  images, 96
  numbering, 96
  opening, 80–81
  page formatting, 95
  paragraph formatting, 95
  printing, 82–83
  quality, 5
  saving, 78–79
  spell-checking, 97
  synonyms, 97
  text, editing, 84–87
  text effects, 95
  type size, 94
  typeface, 94
  types, 79
  word processor, creating, 94–97
dot pitch, 38
drop-down list boxes, 74, 77
DVD drives
  copying to, 21
  defined, 14
  DVD-R, 30
  DVD-ROM, 30
  DVD-RW, 30
  in purchase selection, 37
  speeds, 30
  types of, 30
  using, 62–63
DVDs
  contents, displaying, 63
  external, 62
  inserting, 62, 63
  menus and, 63

E

educational software, 41
e-mail. *See also* Internet
  accounts, 172
  address book, 175
  addresses, 174–175
  advantages, 172
  contacts, 173
  defined, 139
  etiquette, 180–181
  folders, 173
  functioning of, 172
  introduction to, 172–173
  programs, 173
  video, 115
e-mail messages
  abbreviations, 177
  attachments, 177
  checking for, 178
  composing, 176–177
  courtesy copies, 177
  defined, 173
  error-checking, 176
  flames, 181
  forwarding, 179
  receiving, 178–179
  replying to, 179, 181
  smileys, 177
  spam, 178, 216–217
  storing, 179
  viruses, 178, 218–219
Enter key, 53
ergonomic keyboards, 54
ergonomics, 47
errors, hard drive, 200–201
Esc key, 52
etiquette, e-mail, 180–181
expandability, 43
external hard drives, 28
external hardware. *See* peripherals

F

files
  backing up, 206–207
  cleaning up, 204–205
  copying, 88
  defined, 22
  deleting, 91
  instant messaging, sending/receiving, 185
  moving, 89
  renaming, 90
  unnecessary, 204
finances, monitoring, 6
Firefox, 158

Index

Index

Index